on track ...
Roy Wood

The Move, ELO & Wizzard

every album, every song

James R Turner

SONIC**BOND**

sonicbondpublishing.com

Sonicbond Publishing Limited
www.sonicbondpublishing.co.uk
Email: info@sonicbondpublishing.co.uk

First Published in the United Kingdom 2020
First Published in the United States 2021

British Library Cataloguing in Publication Data:
A Catalogue record for this book is available from the British Library

ISBN 978-1-78952-008-8

Typeset in ITC Garamond & ITC Avant Garde
Printed and bound in England

Graphic design and typesetting: Full Moon Media

on track ...
Roy Wood

The Move, ELO & Wizzard

every album, every song

James R Turner

sonicbondpublishing.com

Acknowledgements

I would like to dedicate this book with love to Charlotte,
who has probably heard far more Roy Wood over the last few
months than ever she thought she would!

Thanks Stephen and Huw at Sonicbond
for the opportunity to write this book.

I would also like to thank everyone whose let me loose on
their websites and mags over the past 26 years
& all the good folks at BEM.

on track ...
Roy Wood

Contents

Introduction

This book is about the career of one man – Roy Wood – and the numerous bands and musical projects he had his hand in from 1965 to the present day. Roy was responsible for a string of chart hits from the 1960s onwards and during this time, he turned psychedelic pop into chart-topping singles, reinvented rock and roll, defined 'Glam' and – along the way – he created one of the great, perennial Christmas hits.

His career started with The Move, and he moved on to create The Electric Light Orchestra, Wizzard, The Wizzo Band and Helicopters, in the meantime touching on genres such as pop, rock, progressive rock, folk, psychedelia, glam rock, jazz and doo-wop. To say he is one of Britain's greatest songwriters is no exaggeration, and yet, since the early 1980s, his legacy has been poorly served by a series of compilation albums. Despite some recent reissues, swathes of his back catalogue are currently unavailable on CD, and it took until 1997 for The Move's material to be gathered together in a proper retrospective box set and for the albums to be remastered.

In this book I will look at all the albums and singles recorded by The Move, Roy Wood, Wizzard, The Wizzo Band and Helicopters, and in an appendix, we will round off the story by examining the formative years of Roy's friend and colleague Jeff Lynne with The Idle Race before his membership of The Move in 1970. But this isn't just the story of Roy Wood, The Move, the Electric Light Orchestra and Wizzard; it's a story of cultural change; the transition from pirate to broadcast radio; from the swinging sixties to the striking seventies and flower power to the three day week. In a sense, my own story parallels Roys, as while I grew up, I was far more interested in the classic rock and pop of the 1960s and 1970s than in that of the 1990s, the music of my own generation. With the proceeds of my paper round, I would go to record fairs and junk markets and buy all the old vinyl and singles that those of my Dads age had got rid of when they upgraded to CDs. Now I pick up CDs cheaply when people sell them to go back to their vinyl!

But it was progressive and psychedelic music to which I was most drawn. The starting point for me were The Beatles, followed by The Move, ELO, the Strawbs and Mike Oldfield – the contents of my parent's record collection – but I felt this music spoke to me more than the music of my generation did. This music had depth and emotion, but it was the wonderful gatefold vinyl, providing an immersive experience, that excited me the most. The one band whose music I have had a life-long love for was The Move, not to mention the songwriting talents of Roy Wood throughout his solo and band careers. Woody is one of the great British songwriters, and we'll celebrate his music in this book.

1. The Move 1965 to 1968

Formed from the cream of the top club bands from Britain's second city Birmingham, The Move comprised five ambitious and talented musicians. In their respective bands, they could have ruled clubland in Birmingham for the rest of their careers. However, they wanted more, and so The Move were formed. From Carl Wayne and the Vikings, came Carl Wayne (vocals) Chris 'Ace' Kefford (bass, vocals) and Bev Bevan (drums), joined by Trevor Burton (guitar, vocals) who was playing with Danny King. First to get the call from Burton and Kefford (the initial instigators of the group) was Roy Wood (guitar, vocals) who had been playing with Mike Sheridan's Lot, aka Mike Sheridan's and The Knightriders. Wood's replacement in that band, a young guitarist/songwriter called Jeff Lynne, will join us later.

Interestingly, according to his notes for *The Move Anthology 1966-1972* by Mark Paytress, first in line for the drum seat was Midlands-based drummer John Bonham, who declined the gig. Imagine how different musical history could have been if he'd joined The Move rather than Led Zeppelin. Pretty soon, the new band, named after the fact they had all made 'The Move' from different Birmingham bands, were making waves on the local scene and before long promoter Tony Secunda signed them to his management company. Having already made his mark with the Moody Blues, Secunda and producer Denny Cordell now had a new project.

The band had a lot to offer. First of all, they had five-part vocal harmonies, and their stage show was violent and explosive. Indeed, after their residency at the Marquee ended, the band trashed the place. They also had a 'gangster' image as a gimmick, which some band members enjoyed more than others. But most of all, they had the songwriting skills of Roy Wood. This made The Move a potent musical force, and they began building a powerful following across the country with their live shows. Denny Cordell and engineer Gerald Chevin helped translate the band's stage show and Wood's sublime pop songs, into a successful string of hit singles, followed by a debut album.

This album, unfortunately, was delayed due to the theft of the master tapes which were then found to be unusable, the delay resulting in the band failing to capitalise on the success of their initial singles. So, before we look at that first long-player, let's examine their three singles that hit the charts during the year of 1967, a year that was to have a mammoth cultural, musical and sociological impact on pop culture and indeed twentieth-century history. Sadly, The Move failed to take advantage of all this cultural excitement.

Early Singles
'Night Of Fear' b/w 'Disturbance'
Decca Single
Written by Roy Wood
Produced by Denny Cordell

Personnel:
Roy Wood: guitar, vocals
Bev Bevan: drums
Carl Wayne: Vocals
Trevor Burton: guitar, vocals
Chris 'Ace' Kefford': bass, vocals
Original UK release: 9 December 1966
Highest UK Chart Position: 2
Currently available on *Move – Deluxe Edition* on Esoteric

This debut single encapsulates the sound of The Move as they made the transition from a well-regarded, potent live band to fully-fledged chart stars. This eclectic and exciting debut made the top ten in the UK but did not quite hit the top spot. In its (just under) three minutes, it demonstrates the art of how to make a great single. From the nagging bass riff utilising the '1812 Overture', borrowing classical motifs would be a theme that would dominate Roy's songwriting ideas for a brief but important period of time later down the line, the insistent guitar work from Wood and Burton and the harmony vocals from Kefford, Wood, Wayne and Burton, this was the song that introduced Roy Wood as a songwriter. It is also slightly sinister. Lyrics like 'Silent night has turned to a night of fear' are the flip side of the psychedelic dream, a nightmare trip of dark visions. Propelled by the harmony vocals, these lyrics seem to suggest a trip gone wrong. Yet, apparently, Roy Wood never took drugs, preferring to write dark fairy stories, similar indeed to some of the surreal images conjured by Pink Floyd's Syd Barrett. The song ends with the chorus 'Just about to flip your mind, just about to trip your mind', so there was no wonder there were plenty of drug connotations hanging around the band.

B-side 'Disturbance' continues the theme. It features some odd characters, discusses the concept of the brain not quite working right, and suggests that maybe a stay in Cherry Blossom Clinic will be in order. It is interesting how this theme runs through many of the band's songs. The track is driven by the powerhouse drumming of Bevan, giving it a foot-stomping, soulful r'n'b sound not unlike the driving pulse of 'Keep on Running' by the Spencer Davis Group. It goes rather 'Hammer Horror' at the end, with some strange echoing effects. If anyone was tripping to this, there's a suggestion that the experience might not end well. Wayne and Wood alternate lead vocals, while the harmonies, suggesting a darker version of The Beach Boys, help hold this together. It's not hard to see why this song ended up as the B-side, and while it's not a bad track, it's not one of their classic tunes.

'I Can Hear The Grass Grow' b/w 'Wave Your Flag And Stop The Train'
Decca/Deram single
Written by Roy Wood
Produced by Denny Cordell

Personnel:
Roy Wood: guitar, vocals
Bev Bevan: drums
Carl Wayne: vocals
Trevor Burton: guitar, vocals
Chris 'Ace' Kefford': bass/Vocals
Original UK release: 31 March 1967
Highest UK Chart Position: 5
Currently available on *Move – Deluxe Edition* on Esoteric

'I Can Hear the Grass Grow' is a full-on, lush, psychedelic epic and one of the great British psych singles from 1967. It contains some wonderfully surreal lyrics, entirely in keeping with the times. Although it shows how adaptable Wood was a songwriter, it is also where the split personality of The Move started to show, as, in concert, they were a ferocious and powerful heavy rock band, while on record that spirit was toned down. Instead, they pulled back some of that intensity and used studio magic to craft some sublime seven inches. However, this contrast would never fully be resolved, causing the band to fracture slowly.

When we look at the personalities in the band, the fact that there are four vocalists, providing some wonderful harmonies – as we hear in this famous song, a strong-willed frontman in Carl Wayne, a songwriting genius in Roy Wood, plus the considerable musical abilities of Bevan, Burton and Kefford, means that it's no wonder they made such a massive impact. However, it's also a surprise that they managed to stay together as long as they did.

With the twin guitars of Burton and Wood, the backbeat of Bevan and Kefford, and Wayne upfront, this was a mighty sonic arsenal and one deployed to its full on this single. The song contains some pulsating beats, powerful riffs and some terrific harmonies, matched with suitably 'out there' lyrics and this mixes The Move's heavier r'n'b roots with the burgeoning psych scene. Many bands were trying this approach at the time, and here we see The Move doing it better than anyone, as they manage to bridge the gap between blues and psych.

'Wave your flag and stop the train', however, is a very derivative track in the style of *Help* era Beatles. With its plodding drum and bass, plus its guitar licks, this is a cheerful tale about a girl trying to kill herself by jumping from a train and it is a B-side if ever there was one. It has the sound of a song recorded as a fleshed-out demo with the band not quite knowing what to do with it. It's not a bad song, just a bit of a plod, and ever so slightly in awe of The Beatles. I doubt many people flipped it over too often after listening to 'I Can Hear the Grass Grow'.

'Flowers In The Rain' b/w '(Here We Go) Round The Lemon Tree'
Decca/Deram single
Written by Roy Wood
Produced by Denny Cordell

Personnel:
Roy Wood: guitar, vocals
Bev Bevan: drums
Carl Wayne: vocals
Trevor Burton: guitar, vocals
Chris 'Ace' Kefford': bass, vocals
Original UK release: 25 August 1967
Highest UK Chart Position: 2
Currently available on *Move – Deluxe Edition* on Esoteric

The Move's third single also appeared on their debut album and showed that The band could have at least some luck, as Tony Blackburn played it as the first single on the new national BBC radio network, *Radio One*. It wasn't actually the first track played, as George Martins *Radio One* theme, the appropriately-titled 'Theme One' opened proceedings, but according to Blackburn he just grabbed the first single on the pile and this was it. Tony Secunda tried a bold PR stunt by issuing a postcard advert for the album, complete with a scurrilous rumour, that had been around for years and never adequately answered one way or the other, about the then Prime Minister Harold Wilson and his personal secretary Marcia Williams. As a result, Wilson sued the band, causing them to forfeit their royalties for the single, in perpetuity, to charities of Wilson's choice. This is a ruling still in force today, which means that despite this being one of their biggest hits so far, songwriter Roy Wood has never seen a penny for it, or it's B-side. At just over two minutes long, with its opening thunder, wonderful guitar work and wistful lyrics, this can justifiably be said to be Roy Wood's first bona fide classic single. It still sounds fresh and otherworldly today, as Cordell uses all his production skills to match Wood's lyrical textures and sonic palette.

Unsurprisingly, there were plenty of suggestions at the time that The Move were a drug band, particularly with the dream-like sonics and those sublime harmonies. Indeed, it lays down markers for the different areas that Roy Wood's songwriting would take him. With Wood's knack for a catchy melody, it is one of The Moves definitive singles and – quite simply – a fantastic record. It is one of those songs that is difficult to tire of, even though it helped kick start a radio station that was originally designed to take the pirate radio stations off the air and, thus, helped legitimize a cultural movement. Alternatively, it could be said that when the BBC launched *Radio One*, it was where 'the man' took control of the counter culture for the first time and started the move to mass-manufactured musical styles, pushing against everything that the underground movement was designed to promote. Perhaps this is one of the last cries of that rebellion, as pop music didn't sound as vibrant in the 1970s, and in the era's that followed. Compared to the 1960s, today's pop music sounds positively moribund. But this is music that is full of life and lyrics that float along with little or no real meaning. This, of course, is all part of the charm. Not for the first time, however, would The Move have an open goal, and then put the ball in the back of their own net and due to the delays in releasing the debut album, they failed to capitalise on the momentum that these early singles generated.

The flip side, '(Here We Go) Round The Lemon tree' was another song destined to end up on the delayed debut album. It is another piece of Wood whimsy, with nursery rhyme lyrics subverting the norm slightly, a tale of an odd girl with a lemon tree sounding more like something that Birmingham compadres The Idle Race would write. It's was no surprise that they recorded a cover of it, although that version was lost as radio stations started playing The Move version as the B-side to such a successful single. It has a rocking, if slightly twee tune and when placed alongside it's more illustrious A-side, it does sound like filler, or at least a writer experimenting with different styles to see which one fits best. That said, the string arrangement by Tony Visconti and the harmony vocals do stand out positively. However, this isn't the greatest track by the band and there are some far greater tunes scattered across the debut. Indeed some of the songs originally lost in the studio – only appearing during the extensive re-mastering and reissue projects of 2008 and 2016/17 – are superior.

As the Summer Of Love turned to winter and 1968 began, there was still no sign of the debut album. The next single, another cut that would end up on the album, was the band's last single release to feature the talents of Kefford on bass, who sadly left the group, another unlucky casualty to acid in the 1960s.

'Fire Brigade' b/w 'Walk Upon The Water'
Decca/Deram single
Personnel:
Roy Wood: guitar, vocals
Bev Bevan: drums
Carl Wayne: vocals
Trevor Burton: guitar, vocals
Chris 'Ace' Kefford': bass, vocals
Written by Roy Wood
Produced by Denny Cordell
Original UK release: 6 January 1968
Highest UK Chart Position: 3
Currently available on *Move – Deluxe Edition* on Esoteric

The bands 4th top-five single showed that there was still traction and momentum in the single charts for the band, despite the delays in the debut album being released. Both these tracks would also appear on that record, so we will look at them in that context.

The Move (album)

Personnel:
Roy Wood: guitar, vocals
Bev Bevan: drums
Carl Wayne: vocals
Trevor Burton: guitar, vocals
Chris 'Ace' Kefford': bass, vocals
Produced by Denny Cordell for Straight Ahead Productions with string, brass and woodwind arranged by Tony Visconti.
Released on Regal Zonophone in April 1968
Currently available on *Move – Deluxe Edition* on Esoteric
Highest UK Chart Position: 15

The Move's debut album is housed in wonderfully psychedelic artwork from Dutch collective, *The Fool* and features a fantastic coloured montage of the band on the back, which was brilliantly reproduced in the poster included with the Esoteric reissue from 2016. Astonishingly, it was their only album release to chart and was the culmination of their first two years work. The bulk of the album is made up of Roy Wood originals, with a smattering of cover versions taken from the bands incendiary live set. It contains a dazzling array of styles and musical approaches, showing Wood's versatility as a songwriter, and the wide range of influences that each member brought to the table. I first owned this album back in the mid-1990s, when it was difficult to find, and I enjoyed straight away. It's fuzzy blend of controlled aggression, and psychedelia caught the mood I was in and I updated my vinyl copy when *The Movements 30th Anniversary* box set came out. Later, having parted ways with that version and not replaced it, the Esoteric Recordings copies of this and *Shazam* provided worthy replacements. This three-disc re-master is hugely impressive, taking the original remasters from 2007, adding the stereo mixes on disc two, and rounding the whole set out with a collection of BBC radio sessions from the period January 1967 to January 1968 showing the nascent Move's muscle and aggression as a live unit.

It is impossible to underestimate how important this album was to the development of Roy Wood as a songwriter. The contrary nature of The Move, with such diverse musical influences, would eventually become the band that made *Message From the Country,* a totally different beast from the music created by the original line up. This comprehensive three-disc remaster from Esoteric presents everything that the band recorded from 1966 to 1968, complete with some fantastic live radio sessions from Birmingham local radio (where they are charmingly introduced as 'Carl Wayne's new band') to BBC sessions and archive interviews with Carl.

The album remains one of the great examples of the collision of rhythm and blues and psychedelia, and while the band were not as 'far out' as contemporaries like Pink Floyd, it remains a classic British album, now over fifty years old.

'Yellow Rainbow' (Wood)

The opener starts with some wonderfully fuzzy guitar from both Wood and Burton. Indeed the twin guitar approach works well across this whole album. With call and response lyrics, each member of the band sings lead and harmonises in this post-apocalyptic tale of the mythical Yellow Rainbow – a dystopian sci-fi story set to song. Menacing bass and intensely powerful percussion from Bevan help drive Wood's narrative, as the band discusses a solution to humanity's salvation after a nuclear apocalypse. With 1968 being a mere five years after the Cuban missile crisis, and the arms race escalating, it's no surprise that post Second World War narratives were popular in all areas of popular culture. It does mark the song out as very much of its time, but it is a great opening salvo to the album.

'Kilroy Was Here' (Wood)

All the best songwriters pull inspiration from their surroundings, and this wonderfully written and observed song is in the mould of those very English-style songs which writers like Ray Davies or Paul McCartney were adept at conjuring during the 1960s. With a wonderfully percussive beat, and some jangling guitar reminiscent of The Byrds, interplaying wonderfully with Keffords bass, it tells the story of the mythical 'Kilroy'. 'Kilroy Was Here' was a viral motif of graffiti from the 1940s onwards, and here our narrator speculates about his identity using wonderful rhyming couplets, as well as commentating on the fact the Kilroy seems to get around a lot. It's a very English piece of storytelling, with plenty of those typical Move harmony vocals, and some thundering bass work from Kefford.

'Here We Go Round The Lemon Tree' (Wood)

See discussion with the 'Flowers In The Rain' single.

'Weekend' (Bill & Doree Pos)

Harking back to The Move's stage shows, this is pretty much a straight cover version with Trevor Burton giving it his all, as they reinterpret the Eddie Cochran classic from an earlier era of rock and roll. Within a few years, Wood would go on to write his own rock and roll homages, showing his love of that era.

'Walk Upon The Water' (Wood)

This is a folky track, and the latest re-master really accentuates all the harmony vocals, with musical embellishments that were difficult to pick up on previously. Bevan delivers some wonderfully powerful drumming and matched with Keffords bass, they make a formidable rhythm section, while the whole band give great vocal performances. This cheerful story tells of a group of friends who, while inebriated, decide to go for a walk upon the water, with the chorus sung in a deliberately English accent, while the bugle in the fade-out nods towards the Beatles *Sgt Pepper.*

'Flowers In The Rain' (Wood)
See the discussion of the track as a single.

'Hey Grandma' (Jerry Miller and Don Stevenson)
Another refugee from The Moves exhilarating stage shows, this song is their
take on the Moby Grape classic. As was so common with bands of that era, if
they didn't have enough original songs for an album, they would throw in a
couple of cover tracks from their stage show. With all the time taken to record
this album, it made sense to drop in a couple of old school favourites and this
is a sparky performance, as you'd expect from playing this live so often, with
some great piano work by session man Nicky Hopkins.

'Useless Information' (Wood)
As the sleeve notes for the Esoteric records release state, this acutely observed
Wood classic is the composers second favourite track on the album. I can
understand why, as it's another one of the character studies that populate this
record, this time focusing on the subject of hobbies and collectors. Driven by
the post-war financial boom, leisure time had increased and so there was a
mass change in lifestyle and habits, with more houses having gardens, more
people having disposable income and, as a result, a rise of leisure activities.
'Useless Information' is an observation on this phenomena, from autograph
collecting to neighbourhood gossips, this paean to time-wasting is at turns
both sad and satirical. Lyrics like 'it's not hard to see why conversation is
dying' cannily predict the smartphone era, and the fact that we are bombarded
with 'Useless Information' everywhere. This is more than just a song – it is a
warning from history. The band's performance is sublime, awash with harmony
vocals, and some fantastic guitar work. The fade-out is pure 1967, containing a
wonderful bass line from Kefford and has Wood repeating the final chorus. It is
pure pop perfection.

'Zing Went The Strings Of My Heart' (James Hanley)
This song, the final cover version on the album, was a concert staple for the
band. It has Bev Bevan on main vocals, while Keffords second vocal also adds a
great deal. It shows that the band loved having fun and contains a wonderfully
pounding bass solo from Kefford, while the band's harmonies are, as ever,
sublime. It's all great fun, showing how good the band were at reinterpreting
other people's songs. As a live favourite, it's a good choice to include this song
on the album while also showing the direction they would head into on *Shazam*

'The Girl Outside' (Wood)
This is another string-laden ballad, with an arrangement by Tony Visconti,
showing Wood's softer side, a trick he would later hone on songs like 'Whisper
in the Night' and 'Dear Elaine'.
    With a Trevor Burton vocal, this is another one of Wood's 'story' songs, a

poignant reflection of a relationship with all its struggles. It has our protagonist wishing he were with the 'girl outside'.

'Fire Brigade' (Wood)
As was common throughout 1968, a lot of bands were starting to turn their attention back to the first era of rock and roll. This driving rocker from Wood has a fantastic riff, some great harmonies, and yet more exceptional bass and drums from Bevan and Kefford. The siren-like harmonies and the call and answer vocals are magnificent, as is Wood's wonderful way with lyrical phrasing. Add some fantastic soloing, and this is an absolute classic.

'Mist on a Monday Morning' (Wood)
Laden with strings, flutes and harpsichord, this faux renaissance piece foreshadows the ideas that would evolve into the Electric Light Orchestra. It is a rather mournful story, and it is again a character-driven piece. The potent imagery and the counterpoint of tragic lyrics and beautiful melody also foreshadow what bands like the Beautiful South would use much later to great effect. In effect, a Roy Wood solo piece, this song points to elements of his songwriting style that he would hone and refine on later albums.

'Cherry Blossom Clinic' (Wood)
Rounded off this startling debut album, and later reworked to even crazier lengths on *Shazam,* this is the darkest track on the album. There's a real feeling of psychosis, with backward recording, vocal harmonies, some very Beatle-esque trumpets, and a dark and sinister string track. Mixed with Wayne's vocals, this is spectacular and ends the album in real style. This is the darker side of the Summer Of Love, writ large with lyrics like 'lock me in and throw the key away' and the contrast in pace and mood between the verses and chorus, articulating mania in all its forms, and the doom-laden sting driven fade-out is perfection itself.

Bonus Tracks
The album has been enhanced on recent re-issues by stereo mixdowns of the original album, and some unreleased tracks. The stereo mixes do differ slightly from the original mono album; however, it's the bonus tracks on the latest edition that are of most interest. The first three were previously unreleased before this set, and are from the bands very first sessions recorded in 1966 at Ladbroke Sounds Studios, restored and remastered from the original acetate recordings. Even one unreleased Roy Wood song is marvellous, but three unreleased tracks? That's a treasure trove.

'You're the One I Need' (Wood)
This is a slice of prime British R 'n' B, with some great driving guitar and drums. It is worlds away from the psych sound that Roy would later go on to

develop. Instead, it is a piece of soul-inspired 'Brumbeat', similar to most that would be in the clubs during that era and while it doesn't sound much like the band's later singles or albums, it has some great percussive rhythms, an Ace Kefford vocal that suggests Eric Burdon of the Animals, and a really gritty bluesy sound.

'Winter Song' (Wood)

This is more of a folk-driven piece of music. It's acoustic guitar and vocal harmonies suggest bands like The Byrds, with its gentler sound palette. The song gives an interesting insight into how Wood would develop as a songwriter. The imagery he uses suggests poetry put to music, and while the song is simplistic in its structure, it is still effective – the sort of music that bands like Fairport Convention and the Strawbs would go on to make.

'The Fugitive' (Wood)

This is Another folkier track, demonstrating that Roy had been listening to *Rubber Soul* or *Help* by the Beatles. It is particularly reminiscent of 'You've Got To Hide Your Love Away', with the same driving, pounding guitar style and sublime vocal harmonies yet again.
While it is nascent songwriting, it does show a musician who is continuing to learn and is allowing the band room to practice and grow in the studio. While it is not the most essential of tracks, it is a good indication of where the band were heading and the direction in which Roy was developing as a writer.

Of interest amongst the other bonus tracks are:

'Vote For Me' (Wood)

Originally intended to be the B-Side of the 'Cherry Blossom Clinic' single, both were pulled after The Move were sued by Harold Wilson, and as a result 'Vote for Me' was lost until its first appearance on The *Movements* Anthology in 1997. With a call to arms for the disposed and disenchanted, it's cynical voice and wryly observant lyrics, matched to a pounding mixture of psychedelia and rock, has hints of 'Yellow Rainbow' in the production and a rousing Wayne vocal. It's a genuine Move classic and features Roy at his most cynical, as well as being one of those rare tracks by the band where contemporary affairs creep into the lyrics. Stripped bare of the psychedelic fairy tale element, it takes the aggression of the bands live show and channels it effectively onto record.

Previously unreleased until they were mixed down into Stereo in 2007, are a trio of songs recorded for the debut album and not previously released. These are:

'Don't Throw Stones at Me' (Wood)

As this song has an impressive Ace Kefford vocal, it's probably worth pointing out here that at the start Ace was the driving force behind the formation of the band. With his shock of blonde hair, he was as much of frontman as Carl

Wayne while Roy was the one who wrote the songs. So, giving him lead vocals on songs like this played to his strengths. That was the beauty of the first line up of the band, with five unique vocalists, their harmonies and the swapping of lead vocalists was a real highlight of the band's character. Again, this piece is a fabulous slice of Motown-inspired 'Brumbeat', showcasing their roots in the blues and r 'n' b clubs of their home town as they honed their craft. Lyrically, Roy is really on point as Ace puts some real passion and soul into the vocals, while the backing vocals are stunning. Musically, although the song is conventional in its structure, there are some lovely guitar solos and some fine drumming from Bevan.

'Move Intro/Move' (Wood)
This two-part track opens with some typically wonderful vocal harmonies in an a capella style, leading into a pounding piece of driving rock and roll. It contains some fantastic guitar work, stomping bass and has real guts, its lyrics extolling full-on musical hedonism, inspired by the ability of great music and to make you dance. It is a surprise that this track never made it onto the debut album.

The 1968 singles
Following the release of the five-track *Something Else* EP by The Move, which failed to touch the charts, the group were in a state of flux. By this point, they were down to a four-piece following the departure of 'Ace' Kefford, and Trevor Burton had switched to bass. The situation wouldn't be resolved until after the release of their next studio album, 1970's *Shazam*. Even though the third single from their debut album, 'Fire Brigade' had narrowly missed out on the top spot, their subsequent live EP failed to make an impression on the charts, and heading into the summer the band were plagued with behind the scenes disruption, as well as the age-old debate about whether they were a 'singles' or an 'albums' band. Their often raucous live show had, as yet, not been translated onto a studio album.

The only new music released by The Move in 1968 were two singles, which fared very differently in the charts, and showed the extreme differences between the band's identity, and what the individual members wanted from the group going forward.

'Wild Tiger Woman' b/w 'Omnibus'
Written by Roy Wood
Regal Zonophone single
Produced by Denny Cordell
Personnel:
Carl Wayne: Vocals
Roy Wood: Guitar, keyboards, vocals
Trevor Burton: Bass, vocals

Bev Bevan: drums, vocals
Release: 30 August 1968
Highest UK Chart Position: Did not chart
With:
Richard Tandy: Bass on 'Wild Tiger Woman'
Nicky Hopkins: Piano on 'Wild Tiger Woman'
Currently available on *Shazam* On Esoteric

It is more than 50 years since this single was released, and like a lot of music in 1968, after the psychedelic era, heavier sounds were infiltrating the charts, spearheaded by guitar virtuoso Jimi Hendrix and bands like Cream. Bassist Trevor Burton who has been spending time with Traffic and the Jimi Hendrix Experience (both Trevor and Roy were guests on the Hendrix track 'You got me Floating', providing backing vocals) was keen to push The Move into the heavier and harder direction, in keeping with the bands wilder stage shows, rather than their more pop-orientated recordings. The track really rocks, with some great riffing from Roy, the band powering along, via some risqué lyrics and fantastic harmony vocals. The song takes the bands existing sound and ramps up the rock element. In the context of what was to what came later, it still sounds a little tame, but it also sounds fresh and potent, with a wonderful piano work from session man *de jour* Nicky Hopkins.

However, it bombed completely, failing to touch the hit parade, making it a rare commercial misstep from Wood, who was normally so good at reading what the charts wanted. Perhaps The Move were trying to be something they weren't (yet) on this track and confused the public. They were going to get a whole lot heavier. Bev Bevan has said that the B-Side 'Omnibus' should have been the A-side, and it would have been a more logical follow up to 'Fire Brigade'. 'Omnibus' is still rockier, but it has more of the band's trademark harmonies – alternating vocals between the Burton, Wood and Wayne – while Burton's bass playing bounces the track along. Complex and driving, the bass acts almost like a lead guitar, while the extended fade-out has harmonies reminiscent of The Beatles, and some really funky bass. It is a shame that this bonafide Move classic had been relegated to the B-Side of the single and I agree with Bevan in that had this powerful number been the A-side it might well have cracked the charts, instead of being 'lost' until The Move *Anthology* boxed set in 2008, restored it to its rightful place in the band's canon.

'Blackberry Way' (Wood) **b/w 'Something'** (Dave Morgan)
Regal Zonophone single
Personnel:
Carl Wayne: vocals
Roy Wood: guitar, keyboards, vocals
Trevor Burton: bass, vocals
Bev Bevan: drums, vocals

With: Richard Tandy: Harpsichord on 'Blackberry Way'
'Blackberry Way' produced by Jimmy Miller
'Something' produced by Denny Cordell
Release: 29 November 1968
Highest UK Chart Position: 1
Currently available on: **Shazam** (Esoteric)

Compare the fates of the two Roy Wood penned singles that appeared in 1968. 'Wild Tiger Woman', the first really raucous rock track released as a single by The Move, bombed completely, despite the bands best efforts. The song had been an attempt to keep up with the new, heavier kids on the block. Instead of innovating, The Move made a misstep, which following on the lack of success of their *Something Else* EP. All the behind the scenes disruption with changing management and producers meant that by late 1968 the band were struggling, not for the first or last time. Somehow, they always seemed to grab defeat from the jaws of victory. Then came 'Blackberry Way', the quintessential Move track, regarded as one of Roy Wood's finest songs in any era and one which would have a profound impact on the future of the band. Demoed in Roy's mate, Jeff Lynne's, home studio, and enhanced by fellow Birmingham musician Richard Tandy on harpsichord, this is a tale of love and loss, with some wonderful lines in its lyrics: 'See the battlefield of careless sin, lost to the wind'.

Rich with soaring strings, and some wonderful harmony vocals, this song refines everything that went before it. Wood's vocals are full of loss, pain and yearning, while the band are operating at full power here, with Richard Tandy's harpsichord adding a huge amount to the arrangement. With Roy pleading 'what am I supposed to do now?' he could be asking the question about the band he had helped form back in 1965. This seems to be what hit the spot with the record-buying public all those years ago, catching the nation's imagination and giving The Move their only UK number one. It was the first time Roy had topped the charts. The song still soars today and remains an absolute jewel in the bands crown. Like the Beatles 'Hey Jude', this classic never appeared on a studio album, and it's amazing how defining musical statements like this were so often left for the singles chart, and it also helped reinforce the suggestion that The Move were still, at heart, a singles band. The strings, the harmonies, and the working with Jeff Lynne, all pointed towards direction that the band they would take when Jeff joined at the start of 1970, beginning the path that would lead to the Electric Light Orchestra.

The flipside is 'Something', sung by Carl Wayne, a highly emotive and very soulful piece by Birmingham songwriter David Morgan, who Carl had signed to his own Penny Music label. Morgan bought 'Something' to the band, providing a wonderful musical counterpart to 'Blackberry Way', with once again some great harmony vocals from the band, and a wonderfully impassioned vocal from Wayne. There are a couple of interesting bonus tracks on the *Shazam* reissue, including a demo version of 'Something', showing how the song evolved, as well as both 'Wild Tiger Woman' and 'Blackberry Way' live at the BBC. And then, as The Move appeared to have struck gold once again and reclaimed chart glory, tired of the direction the band were moving in, bassist Trevor Burton quit.

2. The Move: 1968 and 1969 Live Recordings

As mentioned previously, the dichotomy between the more refined studio production of The Move and their live sound, and the fundamental schism at the heart of the band, as to whether they were a singles, an album or a live band, remained. Listening to the polish of the debut album, compared with their more potent live performances, it's hard to marry the two versions of the band together and that contradiction struck at the heart of The Move for the majority of their existence. After all, when they started back in 1965, they were considered some of the best musicians on the Birmingham scene, and it's their vibrant and explosive live act, even more so when taken under the wing of Tony Secunda, that got them press, a residency at the legendary Marquee in London and notoriety.

The band's only two live selections released officially were 1968's *Something Else*, originally a five-track EP and now expanded to a full album on the Esoteric 2016 reissue and *The Move Live at the Filmore 1969*, recordings taken from a tape owned by vocalist Carl Wayne and re-mastered up to current musical standards. These two albums contain live recordings from the first three line-ups of The Move and provide an excellent snapshot of what an almighty force they were as a live band.

Somethings Else From The Move (EP and Expanded Reissue)

Regal Zonophone, released June 1968
'So, You Want To Be A Rock And Roll Star' (Roger McGuinn, Chris Hillman) *
'Stephanie Knows Who' (Arthur Lee)*
'Somethin' Else' (Bob Cochran, Sharon Steely)
'It'll Be Me' (Jack Clement)*
'Sunshine Help Me' (Gary Wright)
Personnel:
Carl Wayne: vocals
Roy Wood: guitar, vocals
Trevor Burton: Guitar *, vocals, bass (except *)
Chris 'Ace' Kefford: bass, vocals *
Bev Bevan: drums
Highest UK Chart Position: Did not chart
Recorded at the Marque London * 27 Feb 1968 & 5 May 1968
Produced by Denny Cordell with Tony Visconti for Straight Ahead Productions
Currently Available as bonus tracks on *Something Else from The Move*, released on Esoteric in 2016

Something Else from The Move (2016 edition Esoteric Recordings)

Personnel as previous entry
'Move Bolero',* 'It'll Be Me',*'Too Much In Love' ,* 'Flowers In The Rain', *Fire

Brigade,* 'Stephanie Knows Who',* 'Something Else',* 'So, You Want To Be A Rock And Roll Star',*
'The Price Of Love',* 'Piece Of My Heart', '(Your Love Keeps Lifting Me) Higher And Higher',
'Sunshine Help Me'.
Plus the original EP.
Produced and mixed by Rob Keyloch at Church Walk Studio London
Tracks 1-12 remastered by Nick Robbins and Rob Keyloch
Tracks 13-17 (the original EP) remastered by Ben Wiseman
Recorded live at the Marquee London 27 February 1968* & 5 May 1968,

When The Move boxed set was released celebrating 40 years of the band in 2008, the *Something Else* concerts were finally tidied up and reissued as part of that set. Having been something of a 'holy grail' for Move completists, they had been shunted around as bonus tracks on different albums, and never given the re-mastering or indeed respect, that they were due. It was released originally as an EP – in other words, something quick and easy to put out to keep the band's momentum going. But being neither single nor album, and originally containing cover versions, it got lost in translation and could be considered a step back for the band. The excellent reissue from Esoteric puts the concerts back together as one complete album, and, for the sake of completeness, the original mono EP was re-mastered.

Between the first recording in February, and the second night in May, the line up of the band changed with 'Ace' Kefford leaving due to the deterioration in his mental health caused by his overuse of acid. Trevor Burton switched to bass from guitar, so this really captures the band in a state of flux. The release of their debut was sandwiched between these two concerts, but it is clear that this is a far more aggressive band in action than the debut would have you believe.

Of course, as with a lot of bands of from this era, the studio albums couldn't be reproduced on stage, and instead of doing what the Beatles did, and abandoning live performances altogether, The Move carried on with their set from before they started having hits, which combined rhythm and blues staples and other tunes popularised locally. The album does show what a formidable live act they had become by this point, and even though they had had a spate of hits and had many quality songs of their own, the sets here are dominated by covers. Blistering versions of 'Something Else and 'Sunshine Help Me' were stand out tracks on the EP, and 'cleaned up' they sound amazing, while the only hits played, 'Flowers in the Rain' and 'Fire Brigade', have a harder edge to them than their recorded versions. The opening track, instrumental 'Move Bolero' is nothing more than an intro track before the full band launches into a rousing version of 'It'll Be Me'. The full version of Move Bolero, one of Wood's instrumental pieces, can be found on the second disc of the debut album re-master. The four-part harmonies from the original line up, give some real power, and the dual guitar work of Wood and Burton really give some raw energy to the band's performances. Kefford and Bevan play with real energy.

Kefford's departure was, in a lot of respects, the catalyst for the problems The Move faced later, as Burton's switch to bass pushed more emphasis on Wood, who was originally happier writing the songs and leaving Wayne as the frontman. Wood ended up singing more of his own songs, which led to less emphasis on Wayne. The soul songs really showcased Wayne's vocal prowess, while the heavier elements that typified the band's live performances were showcased in 'Flowers in the Rain' and 'Fire Brigade'. Remarkable versions of 'Piece Of My Heart' and 'The Price Of Love' give a real indication of the bands diverse influences and show them at the peak of their live powers. In the first three years of life, the band had worked the clubs, learning the ropes and played their way from provincial Birmingham outfit to national success and a residency in London. This album encapsulates the sheer power and strength of the band. The issue would be the complex set of influences within the band, meaning that they never really decided what they wanted to be and it wasn't until Roy Wood and Jeff Lynne were running The Move that there was a clarity of vision. However, part of the band's charm was this crazy, freewheeling approach to music and that comes across superbly in this vibrant live document.

The Move Live At The Filmore 1969 (album)

Personnel:
Carl Wayne: lead vocals
Roy Wood: all guitars, vocals
Bev Bevan: drums, percussion
Rick Price: bass guitar, vocals
Right Recordings/New Movement Right116
Recorded in 1969, released in 2012
Disc 1. 'Open My Eyes' (Todd Rundgren), 'Don't Make My Baby Blue' (Barry Mann, Cynthia Weil), 'Cherry Blossom Clinic Revisited' (Wood), 'The Last Thing On My Mind' (Paxton), 'I Can Hear The Grass Grow' (Wood)
Disc 2. 'Fields Of People' (Wyatt Day and Jon Pierson), 'Goin' Back' (Gerry Goffin, Carol King), 'Hello Susie' (Wood), 'Under The Ice' (Todd Rundgren).
Additional night performances:
'Introduction', 'Don't Make My Baby Blue', 'Cherry Blossom Clinic Revisited', 'The Last Thing On My Mind', The Move's USA Tour Recalled By Bev Bevan.
Recorded live at the Fillmore West San Francisco October 17 and 18 1969.
Tape restored by Rob Keyloch at Church Walk Studio. Re-mastered by Nick Robbins at Sound Mastering. Licensed exclusively from Sue Wayne.

Recorded during The Move's legendary shows in America, this is an absolute gem – the last gift to Move fans from the late Carl Wayne. He had kept the tapes of the bands shows at the Fillmore shows, hoping that, one day, technology would catch up to allow them to be re-mastered and presented to the world. These shows were a huge contrast from the cabaret circuit the band had been working in the UK, and it gave them an opportunity to flex their muscles on stage.

On the album, the band showcase the *Shazam* album, live and loud, complete with progressive interpretations, long and wild solo's and – best of all – the magnificent voice of Carl Wayne. This is something of an essential document for Move fans, as prior to the New Movement/Right Recordings issue in 2012, none of this had been released – or indeed heard – since the night it was performed. Due to the scarcity of Move live recordings, when this album was issued, it was warmly welcomed by fans, as the *BBC Sessions* had been released briefly before being deleted and *Something Else* wasn't available at this point. As a result, this was the first complete concert released in the band's history. This shows the boys in heavy, proto-progressive mode and see's them take on and wildly reinterpret some west coast classics, amongst them a couple of Todd Rundgren originals (he later repaid the favour in his band The Nazz, by covering 'Do Ya') as well as turning their own 'I Can Hear the Grass Grow' into a ten-minute, manic freak-out, complete with improvised guitar work and real power from Bevan and Price – whose role in this period of The Move has always been somewhat overlooked. With Trevor Burton having departed, Wood picks up the slack putting together some astonishing solos. You can really hear the influence of power trios like the Jimi Hendrix Experience and Cream, with the added benefit of Carl Wayne on vocals. His foresight in keeping these tapes, and that of his wife Sue and son Jack for letting them be released, allow a fantastic insight into what a full-throttle, high octane live band The Move in 1969 were. They were a band in flux in the studio, but on stage, they were a dynamic and explosive live act that had toned down a lot of the previous theatrics and honed their performance perfectly.

3. The Move: The Shazam Era

From The Moves' debut album in 1968 to their second long-player released in February 1970, The Move had undergone dramatic personnel changes. After the flop of The Move EP *Something Else*, and the group's only number one 'Blackberry Way', bassist Trevor Burton also quit, fearing the band were heading in too poppy a direction. He was replaced by bassist Rick Price from Birmingham band Sight and Sounds, who would play on the next two albums, adding some stability to the band's rhythm section. The battle for the heart of The Move is writ large across this entire album. The band were earning a good living on the cabaret circuit, which Carl Wayne relished, and Rick Price was used to, but Bev Bevan and Roy Wood wanted to try to get back to their roots, and this dichotomy was represented on this second album. Their debut had been a mixed bag of covers, singles and Roy Wood originals, which, while musically exciting, wasn't as cohesive as it might have been. The questions remained. What sort of band were The Move?

1969 was a turbulent year for the group, with management problems, lack of record company interest and a badly-organised tour of America as part of a heavy live schedule.

The band were let down on the tour by lack of organisation and record label support. However, the tour was a phenomenal success musically, with the set made up of the majority of the material that appeared on *Shazam*. With the 'west coast' vibe infecting the band's sound, the only big hit they played was 'I Can Hear the Grass Grow' (a phenomenal version of which can be found on *The Move Anthology 1966-1972* – Salvo 2008). The double CD live set shows the band off in fine form.

These American influences probably go some way to explaining that while the *Shazam* album was not a commercial success either in the UK or in the USA, it's blend of rock and progressive elements helped it gain it an underground cult following in America, to the extent that 1990s underground band The Shazam named themselves directly after the album. In the end, all the contradictions apparent in The Move were distilled into *Shazam*, which, ironically, in hindsight, is often viewed as the bands best and most consistent album. On the sleeve notes of the latest edition (Esoteric Recordings 2016) Bev Bevan says 'I still love that album, all those gorgeous harmonies draped over those hard rock arrangements. It's The Move's best LP.'

Split down the middle, the album has three Roy Wood originals on side one and then three covers on side two, adding some coherence to the sound, and showcasing the two sides of the band. This compromise was Carl Wayne's idea and provides some structure to the album. Also, as was common throughout the 1960s, the album doesn't contain the only single released by this line up in 1969, the poppier Roy Wood penned 'Curly', which despite its charms, would have stood out badly on the album itself. So, despite its long gestation period, *Shazam* is an incredibly enjoyable record, helped by the fact that the bulk of the material had been 'road tested', and that during the recording period the interpersonal issues that had plagued the band, had settled down somewhat – for the time being at least.

The contemporary reviews for *Shazam*, were excellent, but with nothing new from the band throughout 1969, had they lost momentum?

The album, when released, failed to hit the charts, somewhat overshadowed by Carl Wayne's departure and the entry of Jeff Lynne. With news about the new Electric Light Orchestra also making waves, it seemed that The Move were on borrowed time, and with Roy and Jeff focusing on the next single, the comeback 'Brontosaurus', it seemed that *Shazam* had been forgotten by its creators. This is a shame. It's the perfect encapsulation of the late 1960s Move sound; the perfect blend of Wood's storytelling, and the band's knack of reinterpreting cover versions successfully both on record and in concert. Amusingly, as part of the album, Carl Wayne ambushes various members of the public to gauge their opinions on popular music, and these interviews are then interspersed amongst the tracks, creating an interesting and humorous contrast to the serious musicianship on display and showcasing to the band's sense of humour.

The current edition on Esoteric recordings (across two discs) features all the singles from 1968, as well as BBC sessions from that period, showing the band trying out cover versions and songs that would end up on *Shazam,* a huge chunk of which are previously unreleased. They give a good example of how the band were evolving the songs that eventually made the album.

'Curly' (Wood) **b/w 'This Time Tomorrow'** (David Morgan)
UK: Regal Zonophone, released 18 July 1969
US: A&M released July 1969
Personnel:
Carl Wayne: vocals
Roy Wood: guitars, recorders, Vocals
Rick Price: bass, Vocals
Bev Bevan: drums
Produced by Mike Hurst
Highest UK Chart position: 12
Currently available on *Shazam,* released on Esoteric in 2016

'Curly' was the only new record from The Move in 1969, following on from their only UK number one, in 1968's 'Blackberry Way'. Trevor Burton had departed as he felt the band was heading in the wrong direction, and, if he heard this before he left, then he'd have felt right justified. This song was probably the 'poppiest' The Move had ever sounded. What was going on?

Certainly, as a composer and performer, Roy Wood was always keen to try out new things, and experiment with his writing, even if that took him in the way of this light pop tune. Furthermore, the band were desperate to capitalise on the success of 'Blackberry Way' and aim to be commercial – in their singles at least. Either way, this was a curiously slight single, telling its story of Curly, trying to win back his lost love. The *Shazam* booklet sleeve suggests that Bev Bevan hated it and that Carl Wayne wasn't happy with having to sing the chorus of 'Curly, where's your girly, where's she gone?' Yet, musically, it's not a bad song, with some lovely acoustic guitar and a recorder part that does suggest a nursery rhyme, despite a few twee elements to it. There are some wonderful harmonies, the trademark of so many early Move singles, and it has quite a catchy tune – it's very sing-along. Despite his dislike of it, Carl Wayne gives the song his best, and it is his emotive vocals that raise the song beyond blandness. Ultimately, however, it was a very slight record – the sound of a band treading water and trying very hard not to drown.

By this time, Carl Wayne had also moved into music publishing, signing up two Birmingham songwriters, one of whom – Richard Tandy – would become Jeff Lynne's right-hand man in ELO, a role he still fulfils to this day and the other Dave Morgan, would write for The Move. It is his tune, 'This Time Tomorrow', also marking the first time Rick Price had sung on a Move release, that took up the B-side. It's better than the A-side, with a wonderfully laid, west coast back vibe – very 1968. The song has a much more pastoral sound, and Price had an incredibly soulful voice, which was underused by The Move. With a stripped-back production, subtle percussion from Bevan, a beautifully understated solo from Wood, and Price's sinewy bass, the track has a beautiful flow about it. It is an excellent song about breaking up and is full of the loss of romance, sensitively performed by the band, and superbly written by Dave Morgan. Morgan would later go on to join ELO.

Shazam (album)

UK: Regal Zonophone, released 26 February 1970.
USA: released February 1970
Personnel:
Carl Wayne: vocals
Roy Wood: guitars, keyboards, vocals
Rick Price: bass, vocals
Bev Bevan: drums
With:
Tony Visconti: bass on 'Beautiful Daughter'
Produced by Roy Wood, Rick Price and Carl Wayne with Gerald Chevin for Straight Ahead Productions. Recorded at Advision Studios London. String and woodwind arrangements by Tony Visconti
Highest UK chart position: Did not chart
Currently available on *Shazam*, released on Esoteric in 2016

Shazam showcased the two dominant personalities in the band at the time equally, with Roy's songs highlighted on side one, and Carls voice the star of side two. It is a shame that the band couldn't reconcile the differences between

Carl wanting to move in a more adult direction and Roy's desire to create the Electric Light Orchestra. However, part of the creative tension and energy around The Move was the friction created by two competing musical visions – both a blessing and a curse to the band.

The current two-disc remaster(Esoteric Recordings 2016) includes all the A and B sides of the 1968/1969 singles, alternative demo versions and several BBC sessions recorded by both the 1968 and 1969 line-ups, which showcase the different styles of the bands at this time.It includes some really interesting cover versions of songs like the Beach Boy's 'California Girls', Neil Diamond's 'Kentucky Woman' (also given the Deep Purple treatment) and a sublime version of the Simon and Garfunkel song 'Sound of Silence'. These bonus sessions help fill in the gaps between the 1968 singles and the 1970 *Shazam* album and provide an interesting picture as to how the band were developing up to that point.

Carl Wayne moved on to session work, acting (including a memorable stint as the narrator in Willy Russell's seminal musical *Blood Brothers*) before joining the Hollies and sadly passing away in 2004. If any one record can be said to represent Carls legacy from his time in The Move, it is *Shazam*. It stands as his finest work with the band.

'Hello Susie' (Wood)

This Roy Wood song opened the first album of material from The Move since their psychedelic debut hit the shops in April 1968. While there had been singles, and a live EP, this album was far too long in the making to capitalise on the success of that initial album, and with a different line up to the debut – no Move studio album featured the same personnel – and a totally different sound, anyone who'd been expecting 'Night of Fear' part two would have been surprised by the musical onslaught that *Shazam* represents. This whimsical story of Wood meeting a girlfriend from the train, upstaging a visit from the Queen, is typical of Roy's songwriting style and has some nice lyrical touches and word-play. The song had already been recorded by Amen Corner, who took it into the top ten in 1969, and their version was a slice of prime psychedelic pop reminiscent of The Move themselves from 1967/68. Here, however, with the help of Wood's harsher vocals and a really aggressive take on the riff, this was a short, sharp, shock to kick the album off.

With a classically inspired, heavy middle section, Bevan's drumming and Prices bass riffs both superb and Wood practically rasping out the vocals in a harsh and curt fashion, this is the perfect blend of old and new Move, taking the best parts of the debut album – the vocal harmonies, the use of melody, Wood's well-observed lyrics – and combining these with the direction the band were going. It has the heavier tone, the use of more intricate classically infused ideas and Wood more to the fore as a vocalist. This neatly encapsulates the musical crossroads that The Move were standing at in one four-minute 51 seconds blast of pure energy.

'Beautiful Daughter' (Wood)

This is one of Roy's finest ballads, sung to perfection by Carl Wayne, who was the soul of The Move for so long during its early years. His smooth and versatile vocals provided the perfect foil to Wood's lyrical vision, and while his gentler tone was more suited to the cabaret circuit than the rest of the band, that doesn't diminish anything that he brought to The Move. With Trevor Burton departing, the emphasis moved back to Wayne's vocals and ability as a frontman, as evidenced by the *Filmore Live 1969* album. The song provides a rare moment of calm amongst the heavier parts of the album, and with a lush score and bass performance from Tony Visconti, the production and performance on this piece are beautiful.

The song is another heartbreak story from Wood, and Wayne emotes beautifully as he sings such sublime lyrics as 'your beautiful daughter, made me younger yesterday'. Such wonderful lyricism again shows off Wood's poetic and romantic side. Meanwhile, the string quartet that Visconti arranged and conducted for the sessions brings a vibe, not unlike The Beatles 'She's Leaving Home'. The strings soar to match Wayne's vocals, with a beautifully understated performance from the band. 'Beautiful Daughter' is rightly acclaimed as one of Roy's finest songs with The Move and despite being much more introspective than any of his other originals on this album, it fits the record perfectly. It is a superb testament to the qualities that Carl Wayne brought to The Move, and how much of a multi-faceted performer he was. Mooted to be the most likely single from the album, the departure of Carl Wayne put paid to that idea, sadly.

'Cherry Blossom Clinic Revisited' (Wood)

It is time to check in one more time into 'Cherry Blossom Clinic', a remake of one of the stand out tracks on the debut album. It seems very odd on an album where fifty per cent of the songs are cover versions, to then have one of the band's earlier tracks. Indeed, a revisit to the debut album seems to suggest a paucity of material. As Bevan notes in the sleeve notes to the *Shazam* Remaster: 'The reason the tracks were so long, was because we hadn't got enough material' and a glance at the tracklisting might have made the listener think they had been short-changed slightly. However, this is as radical a revision as there could be, hinting at how the song would sound when played on the American tour. Instead of the original intro, Carl gives a bewildered, spoken word intro in his finest Birmingham accent, before Roy launches in with this heavier and harder retread. This reworking is probably the best way to gauge the difference between the old and the new Move sound, and as the band had evolved, 'Cherry Blossom Clinic' is one song that had also evolved with them. On *Shazam*, the song was stretched out to over seven minutes, further perpetuating the idea that the album essentially compiled from choice cuts from the current live set.

The track begins with a spoken word intro, followed by a heavier reinvention of the familiar song. It then heads off via a familiar trick of Wood's – borrowing classical motifs (in this case Bach and Tchaikovsky) which are then woven into a long, extended coda. With this longer reinterpretation and blend of classical music and traditional rock instrumentation, this was The Moves first steps along the road towards the heavier progressive sound of *Looking On*, as well as the classical leanings of The Electric Light Orchestra.

'Fields Of People' (Wyatt Day and John Pierson)

The opening track on the second side of the album is the first of three non-originals, a cover version of a track by classical rockers Ars Nova. It opens with some lovely acoustic guitar, and Carl Wayne singing some of the vocals from the streets outside Advision studios, talking to passers-by and making it sound it like he's talking to the audience. The chorus has a wonderfully intense acoustic guitar riff, and some sublime harmonies from the band. However, it's Wayne's vocals that drive the verses, singing about love on this very reflective track. The insistent chorus has some great bass work from Price. He mentions in the sleeve notes for *Shazam* that Fields of People '... was one of the first songs I learned when I joined'.

Starting out in a folk-rock vein, the track builds littered with harmonies, spoken word sections and random chat from the London streets, before leading into an extended Indian raga-style closing section, similar to the music George Harrison had created on his *Wonderwall Music* album. Wood's skills on the sitar are showcased, while Bevan and Price keep the beat going, allowing the improvisation to build to a climax. While it's usually considered that *Looking On* was the first full-length progressive rock album by The Move, we certainly find them making steps into the world of progressive music on this album and stretching their own musical boundaries.

'Don't Make My Baby Blue' (Barry Mann & Cynthia Weil)

Opening with a conversation about music with a London Taxi driver, the track bursts into a heavier and far more powerful interpretation of the Barry Mann/Cynthia Weil classic, also covered by both the Shadows and Frankie Laine, who had a hit with the track. A song from the band's cabaret days, Wayne imbues this rendition with all the power and soul that he can muster, while the heavier and more powerfully, insistent riffing from Roy and driving bass make this feel almost like proto-metal, not unlike the kind of reinterpretation of tracks like 'A Little Help from my Friends' by Joe Cocker and Hendrix's version of 'Hey Joe'. With the limitations of the instrumental line up of the band, The Move instinctively knew how to mould those restrictions to make a great cover version with respect for the original song. This is the reason that this half of *Shazam* works so well. The originals have been filtered, refined and interpreted, but made into something that this is unquestionably The Move.

'The Last Thing On My Mind' (Tom Paxton)

The first time I heard this Tom Paxton classic sung as it was written by the original author, was sung a capella in a pub in Northern England. I knew the words, as I knew The Move version, so I was able to join in with the rest of the pub. This song of loss and heartbreak is a masterpiece in whichever genre it is performed. Here it is drenched in guitar and reverb, with slow, instinctive Indian-style guitar phrasing by Wood. The star of the show is once again Carl Wayne, whose idea this track was. He pulls every inch of heartbreak in the song into the vocals, as it builds to its climax. There is also a country-rock vibe that runs throughout this piece, with nods to the heritage of the original song, and you can hear the power and emotion in Carls vocals, as Roy joins in on the chorus, both voices soaring in joyful harmony.

Looking On (album)
Personnel:
Roy Wood: vocals, oboe, slide guitar, cello, guitar, bass and all saxes
Jeff Lynne: guitar, piano, vocals, percussion and drums on 'Feel Too Good'
Rick Price: bass
Bev Bevan: drums and percussion
With:
Doris Troy & PP Arnold: backing vocals on 'Feel too Good'
Produced by Roy Wood and Jeff Lynne except 'Brontosaurus' and 'Lightnin' Strikes twice' produced by Roy Wood
Recorded at Philips Studios London, except 'Brontosaurus' recorded at Advision Studios, London
Released on Fly Records on 1 December 1970
Currently available on *Looking On* (2016 remastered edition) on Esoteric
Highest UK Chart position: did not chart

Singles:
'Brontosaurus' (Wood) **b/w 'Lightnin' Never Strikes Twice'** (Rick Price, Michael Tyler)
Released on Regal Zonophone on 6 March 1970
Highest UK Chart position: 7

'When Alice Comes Back To The Farm' (Wood) **b/w 'What?'** (Lynne)
Released on Fly Records on 9 October 1970
Highest UK Chart position: did not chart

By 1970, Jeff Lynne had left the Idle Race and joined Roy Wood, Bev Bevan and Rick Price in The Move, meaning that, once again, the line up of the band had changed before their previous album had even been released. Even with *Shazam,* the latest long-playing record, Roy Wood and Jeff Lynne were already cooking up their plans to put The Move to bed and change their focus to the new Electric Light Orchestra. However, they still had the small matter of a record deal with Onward Music to consider, not to mention various touring commitments.

The introduction of Jeff Lynne into the band helped Roy Wood immensely. As the main songwriter, he had been responsible for most of the heavy lifting and having a second songwriter, especially one as gifted as Jeff Lynne, was a real weight off his shoulders. This meant that for the first time on a Move album there were two songwriters pulling their weight in the band. *Shazam* had tried very hard to marry up the more progressive nature of Roy Wood's songwriting, and the cabaret-styled leanings of Carl Wayne. It had done this pretty successfully, and by the time the album hit the shelves in February 1970, the band that had recorded it had already split up and moved on from the 'chicken in a basket' circuit to the progressive underground scene.

Listening to this album back to back with *Shazam*, is like the sound of two totally different bands and with Lynne on board, it gave Roy Wood more freedom to push beyond his own musical boundaries, past the traditional pop for which he had become known. *Looking On* is the first time that a Move album has a genuine polish and a coherence running through it, and the first time the live and studio bands completely coincided.

It is without a doubt my favourite album by the band and the first one I ever bought in the early 1990s, on German import, with sleeve notes translated from German back into English which were hilarious, if not very accurate. It reminded me of fellow Birmingham band Black Sabbath. I have bought this album four times. The second time was when it was reissued for The Move's 30th Anniversary in the *Movements* box with the debut album and *Shazam*, thirdly when Salvo re-mastered and reissued it properly in 2008, and now most recently in the double-disc Esoteric edition. It is, without doubt, The Moves heaviest album. Everything is amplified, including the length of the songs, and this is The Move at their most progressive and inventive.

By the time it was released, they had jumped ship to EMI's Harvest label, meaning that the releasing label did nothing to promote the album, and between the success of *Message From The Country* and the rise of the Electric Light Orchestra, it got somewhat lost. Luckily the intervening years have been incredibly kind to *Looking On*, despite the fact that until 2008, The Move's back catalogue had been treated abysmally. The current reissue from 2016 has excellent sound quality, in-depth sleeve notes and for the first time comes complete with a second disc of previously unreleased, contemporaneous BBC live recordings which show how close to the record the live version of The Move were at that point. It includes interviews with Bev Bevan and Roy Wood, incendiary live versions of the title track, the lead single 'Brontosaurus', the previously unreleased Jeff Lynne track 'Falling forever' and a couple of superb versions of the Beatles song 'She's a Woman'. Finally, *Looking On* can be appreciated as one of the great albums by the band, one that doesn't put a foot wrong from start to finish, and one that hooks the listener and doesn't let them go. It's genuinely progressive, allowing Jeff Lynne to unleash his creativity, spurring on Roy Wood, who was finally unshackled from the compromises he had had to take in the previous line ups, creating some of his heaviest music to date.

Of their first three albums *Looking On*, is easily the most coherent Move album and it is significant for several reasons. To begin with, It's the album where Roy took on the mantle of frontman and went on to develop the image that would come to fruition in Wizzard. It introduced Jeff Lynne to the wider public as a huge songwriting talent and finally, it was the first Move album to feature no cover versions at all. The arrival of Jeff Lynne kick-started an intensely creative and musically fulfilling period for the musicians involved over the next two years, which saw The Move bow out with a bang with a late period push of hit singles, an album regarded by some as their finest moment and the launch of the Electric Light Orchestra. *Looking On* deserves to be re-evaluated in this context as the first stepping stones on the road to ELO and Wizzard, as well as being one of the finest albums in The Move catalogue.

'Looking On' (Wood)

This mighty title track introduces itself in a wave of crashing guitar and is nothing like any previous opening to a Move album. This was in the style of openers by bona fide heavy rock bands. Fans that had been listening to the crunchier, guitar-heavy sound of lead single 'Brontosaurus' (of which more below) might have been primed for this. However, for those expecting more of the same from The Move, this was an almighty surprise. Starting with a powerful drum roll from Bevan, this is immediately in hard rock territory, with Lynne and Wood duelling on lead guitar, incorporating time changes and chunky riffs which sweep the listener along. At over seven minutes, it's a full-on epic and in it, the song sheds the final vestiges of both The Moves psychedelic whimsy and their cabaret leanings. Gone, too, are the harmonies and the smooth vocals of Carl Wayne. Instead, this is the moment where Roy Wood steps out to the front, stops being just the songwriter and finally becomes frontman of the band. The piano riff underpinning the beat, and the guitar line that matches Wood's vocal, show that the power The Move could put into their stage shows could be translated onto record. The middle section sees both guitarists echo the riff around, while the song builds into soloing reminiscent of the twin guitar assault of Wishbone Ash. There is a nod to the bands past, as a heavy and intricate sitar solo from Wood rides through an extended coda, while Lynne's piano playing is also a fundamental building block to the success of the track. Rick Price never gets as much credit as he deserves in The Move, but here he is the perfect foil for Bevan, allowing Wood and Lynne free rein to put their musical vision across.

The song showcases Roy's expanding multi-instrumental skills, using his collection of eclectic and eccentric instruments, but he pulls it off in style. The current double-disc edition of *Looking On* also contains an incendiary live version of this performed at the BBC by the four-man band. Stripped back to the new two-guitar, bass and drums line up, this really cuts to the heart of the track and gives it a powerful kick, making it even harder and rawer than it is on record. The live performances on this disc really show the power of the band on stage, operating right at the peak of their 'heavy' period.

'Turkish Tram Conductor Blues' (Wood)

A high-octane twelve-bar blues, Roy shows off his vocal range, on this energetic and complex rocker. It seems quite straightforward until you dig a little deeper, and notice the variety of instruments that Roy plays on here, as well as the interesting little shuffles that Bevan manages to sneak in. The guitar work of both Lynne and Wood is superb and the sax solo from Roy, rising and falling throughout, is the first indication of the direction he would later head in with Wizzard and its various iterations, particularly on the 'lost' album, *Main Street* – but more of that later.

'What?' (Lynne)

'What' was the first Jeff Lynne composition for The Move to be released on an album and it shows just how far Jeff's work had developed from his time in the Idle Race. At 6:42 long, it's probably twice the length of anything he'd recorded with that band. As Jeff's intention in joining The Move was to develop the Electric Light Orchestra idea, his songs on here feel like dry runs for that band's first couple of albums. His piano playing is very much to the fore – something that hadn't been a fundamental part of The Move sound before – and there are some dramatic chord sequences. His higher-register vocals, textured guitar effects and Roy's vocal harmonies, gives a sense of epic dynamics that makes this one of the stand-out tracks on this album. Jeff's songwriting is given space to breathe here, and he shows a great ear for mixing melodies and harmonies in his guitar playing. It was nothing like any Move track before and is perhaps a 'lost' progressive rock highpoint.

'When Alice Comes Back To The Farm' (Wood)

The second single from the album, this catchy, upbeat rocker, failed to dent the charts, probably since the band were on their way out of their Fly deal and off to a lucrative new contract negotiated by one of rock managements most notorious legends, Don Arden. It is another sax driven, hard rock track, with some powerhouse drumming from Bevan and a funky piano riff from Lynne. The cello breaks and woodwind clearly signpost the future of The Moves music, but this is an absolute full-on rock track, with the piano of Lynne, the guitar of Wood and the saxes all duelling with each other as it builds. Another tune that is full of energy and vitality, it rocks out far more than The Move ever had done before. 1970 was the dawning of the age of heavy metal, and bands like Deep Purple, Uriah Heep, Black Sabbath and Atomic Rooster were adapting the hard-edged blues, as a reaction, almost, to the psychedelic movement. Listening to this you can't help but feel that this line up of The

Move, with two songwriters in the band, a penchant for experimentation and a reputation for powerful live shows, wanted their album to reflect their personality, and that's what works so well about tracks like this. There's no compromise. Instead, this is the most honest reflection of the band that had ever been put together on an album.

'Open Up Said The World At The Door' (Lynne)

The second Lynne original kicks off the original side two of the album, clocking in at over seven minutes, showcasing the confidence Lynne had in his newfound freedom. In fact, after the closing 'Feel too Good', it is the longest track on the album. This is definitely Lynne in his progressive period, experimenting and trying sounds that he would refine for the ELO debut. With a two-pronged vocal attack from Lynne and Wood, over Lynne's of driving piano, and a sitar solo from Wood, this track mixes those features with some great work by both Bevan and Price. The bass and piano interlude is particularly good and there's even some oboe from Wood.

At first glance, the track does seem like a section of different songs worked together to create one piece, so that it becomes one of Jeff's early mini-symphonies. It even has a drum solo from Bevan (this was 1970, after all), and an extended coda has some fantastic guitar work. The vocal harmonies here are superb as well, making this one of the most inventive and genuinely progressive songs The Move recorded.

'Brontosaurus' (Wood)

Brontosaurus was the first single release since Summer 1969 and was about as far from 'Curly' as it could possibly be, hitting the top ten in March 1970. Gone are the nursery rhyme lyrics, instead this has another powerful, chugging rock and roll riff, with Roy Wood's vocals over an insistent and repetitive, almost metallic, riff, and a catchy, powerful chorus. However, it wasn't the song that proved the biggest surprise; it was Roy Wood's appearance. This was the start of his 'harlequin' years, which saw him turn up for *Top of the Pops* in full face paint, kick-starting the nascent glam scene in which he was to play a major part. The bonus disc of the 2016 reissue contains the announcements for the BBC Radio sessions and DJ Brian Matthews describes this as The Moves 'new sound'. There's little doubt that the arrival of Jeff Lynne had given The Move a new lease of life, even while, paradoxically, it was clear throughout this period that The Move were on borrowed time, with plans for the Electric Light Orchestra in progress.

However, considering the singles – and album – were supposed to be contract fulfilling, the sheer power and energy of these songs suggest that rumours of their impending demise were greatly exaggerated, as events over the next few years were to prove. This catchy rocker is one of only three tracks on this album that is under five minutes long. The BBC session version slows it down, amps it up, and turns it into something darker, harder and heavier than anything that had previously been produced by the band. It showcases how strong a live act The Move were at this point, and how inventive they could be, even working within the confines of the traditional two guitars, bass and drums format in their live shows. In fact, in a BBC interview also on the bonus disc, Roy cites these restrictions as one of the reasons he wanted to start the ELO project.

'Feel Too Good' (Wood)
This closing nine-minute epic is the pinnacle of the album, mixing the heavier sound and the dextrous instrumentation that had been in evidence throughout the record. It features guest vocals from two of the finest soul singers operating in the UK, Doris Troy and American P. P Arnold. Beautifully soulful, it sounds like nothing else on the album. The track starts with a simple backbeat from Bevan, who, despite describing this album as 'a bit Ploddy' to Mark Paytrees in the sleeve notes for the latest reissue, always gave everything on any track he was involved in, his drumming being a fundamental part of The Move sound. Price's bass follows, then Wood's guitar and Lynne's, piano, and finally Wood's vocals. Building on a relatively simple riff and drum and bass pattern, this is catchy, insistent and probably the best song this line up recorded. The female vocals counterpoint Roy's, the bass and drums are wonderfully funky, and Lynne's adds a sublime piano solo. Given how well each instrument plays its part, it is a surprise that the drum pattern hasn't been sampled by some hip-hop stars, as it is so distinctive. The track also offers up a range of solo's and instead of multi-layered overdubbing, the music is pared down, giving each instrument the chance to breathe. This is the finest example of The Move stretching out on record, culminating in a wonderfully intense and soulful finale. The track clatters to a finish, followed by some wonderful 'doo-wop' harmonies from Lynne, Wood and Bevan, and then we get the 'hidden track'...

'The Duke Of Edinburgh's Lettuce'
'Show us yer lettuce' shouts a member of the band over a jangly, music hall-style piano. It's awash with humour, and, just like the rest of the record, it's not quite what the listener expects.

Bonus Tracks
The most recent re-issues contain various bonus tracks that include alternative studio run-throughs and rehearsals of the different songs on the album, and while there are minor differences in style, it's more interesting to hear how the songs involved. There is nothing fundamentally different enough to warrant further investigation here. However, the B-sides and live versions included on the 2016 edition are worth looking at, briefly.

'Lightin' Never Strikes Twice' (Price, Tyler)
Written by bassist Rick Price and Mike Sheridan, this was the second vocal outing from bassist Price. It is a well-written, power-pop song, reminiscent

of 1969 era Move, and may have alleviated some of the fears from fans of the band, that there was to be yet another change in direction. Price had a knack for a melody and a great voice, but his role in The Move was always overshadowed by the changes in direction and emphasis on the drift towards Electric Light Orchestra project, in which he was never going to be involved. This is a perfect bookend to that earlier part of The Moves story, and while Rick left The Move after *Looking On*, he was to return to working with Roy pretty quickly, becoming bassist in Wizzard.

'Falling Forever' (Lynne)

It's not very often that a 'lost' Jeff Lynne song turns up, but when the archives were being searched for the Esoteric re-issue of *Looking On*, various BBC sessions were discovered, containing some remarkable live versions, including the afore-mentioned, incendiary version of 'Brontosaurus' that is even heavier and more menacing than the single version. There is also a turbo-charged version of 'When Alice Comes Back to the Farm', plus two intense covers of the Beatles 'She's a Woman' that are unrecognisable from the Fab Four's original. Then there is this track. It contains some jangling guitar and harmonies from Wood and Lynne. The song, with great lead vocals from Jeff Lynne, is very reminiscent of The Byrds, while the riffs, solo's and harmonies have all the hallmarks of latter-day ELO about them. With it's more complex guitar parts, and softer, almost country/rock feel, it certainly wouldn't have fit into the tracks on *Looking On*, feeling more like a hybrid of Idle Race and The Move. While it's a shame this wasn't recorded away from the BBC, it's fantastic that this has finally come to light, as there aren't too many previously-lost early Lynne songs out there.

Message From The Country (album)

Personnel:
Roy Wood: vocals, oboe, guitar, steel guitar, bass, clarinet, bassoon and all saxes.
Jeff Lynne: vocals, piano, guitars, electric piano and percussion
Bev Bevan: Drums, percussion and vocals
Produced by Roy Wood and Jeff Lynne
Originally released on Harvest
Released; 4 June 1971
Highest UK Chart position: Did not chart
Currently only available in *Roy Wood The Original Album Series*, Parlophone/ Warner Brother, 2014. Also available on vinyl and to stream or download

Recorded during the same time as the debut ELO album, this is very much the flip side of that album. It takes the complex and intricate songwriting that dominated *Looking On* but strips it right back. While it has been suggested that this is the contractual obligation album – the one that the band 'had' to make – as always, the story is much more complicated than that. Signed to EMI/ Harvest by Don Arden, the band were contracted as both The Move and The Electric Light Orchestra, with the label initially wanting the 'name' band to release more material before the ELO debut hit the stores.

As we have discussed, the dichotomy at the heart of The Move was an unequal balance between the singles and the albums, but *Message from the Country* is where those two aspects of the band were finally reconciled. The songs are much shorter and more concise than its predecessor, any one of which could have been a single. This is what probably made it my least favourite Move album for a long, long time. While I enjoyed the psychedelia of the charming, if wayward, debut and the full-on rock power of *Looking On*, the subtleties in *Message From The Country* passed me by at first. It was originally reissued back in 1994 on the BGO label as a straight album to CD reissue, with vague album notes, and none of the non-album singles or B-sides

Later, I realised that on *Message From The Country*, Lynne and Wood were having fun, relaxing into their songwriting. The bigger pieces belonged in the room marked ELO, and *Message* was a vehicle to send The Move off in style. This album's songs last no longer than they need to, and the studio techniques that Wood – and especially Lynne – had learnt are used to fine effect here. There is even a second vocal outing for Bev Bevan (his first being on The Move debut), and the whole thing sounds more comparable with the pared-down, chilled out vibe of the early 1970s than the manic proto-prog, 'everything but the kitchen sink' sound of *Looking On*. It also follows The Move's 'tradition' of never releasing a studio album with the same line up of musicians.

The album was superbly remastered and reissued in 2005 by EMI, with the bonus of the quartet of singles released throughout 1971 and 1972, showcasing the direction the individual songwriting of both Lynne and Wood was heading in beyond The Move.

Unfortunately, this package is currently available on vinyl it remains unavailable on CD and it is available to stream and download. You can also find good CD copies available online for a not unreasonable price. So the only version that is currently available on disc is the basic album, bundled up in a box with five other albums that feature Roy Wood, which is a really shoddy way to deal with an album as great as this, and incredibly disappointing that it's included in a box set when people might already have versions of the other albums anyway. In particular, if you are discovering *Message* for the first time, you are missing out on the singles that were released around it. Both *Looking On* and *Message from the Country*, my personal favourites, seem more complete, rounded albums, probably because Jeff became a worthy foil to Roy in the songwriting department. Indeed, by this time the band was a trio of Wood, Lynne and Bevan, with an equal partnership between the two songwriters.

This led to a more cohesive approach and with two songwriters in the band. It not only gave them breathing space, but it also spurred each of them to improve and excel. The 1970 to 1972 period was the high watermark in terms of quality for The Move. *Message* isn't Bev Bevans favourite Move album – in the sleeve notes he states '*Message* is probably my least favourite Move album (*Shazam* is my favourite), but it does exude a sense of fun.' Reappraisal suggests that it is one of the band's better albums.

'Message From the Country' (Lynne)

The album starts with a bit of an odd curveball from The Move, a topical – and even more relevant today – track about the impact humankind is having on the environment. Significantly, a Jeff Lynne track was used as the album's title track for the first time. There are also shades of '10538 Overture', with a very similar chord sequence and this also inspired the cover, drawn by Roy, showing him playing a sitar on a mountain – even though he doesn't play that instrument on this album. The band member's faces are in the clouds. The imagery on the cover is none too subtle – the bird is a bomber about to drop his 'load'. Inside, Jeff's songwriting is quite radical, very observational compared to some of his other writing from around the same time. It also includes some fine bass from Roy and some great guitar work from Jeff. Considering they were a trio, the biggest surprise is how huge the sound is, as they utilised every aspect of the studio and Instead of the intense and dense 'wall of sound' that permeates *Looking On*, the production here has a much lighter touch, with the instrumentation and style much more pared-back and intimate. In complete contrast to *Looking On*, where the power and density threaten to overpower some of the songs, here the emphasis is fully on the songwriting itself, and it's interesting to wonder what these songs might have sounded like given the ELO treatment.

'Ella James' (Wood)

Probably the rarest Move single in existence, 'Ella James' was initially released in May 1971 (with 'No Time' on the flip side) but was pulled and replaced with the non-album track 'Tonight' (see below). This Wood rocker is a distant relation to 'When Alice', or 'Hello Suzy', but instead of the bombast of those two songs, this has a more laid back approach. There is more sublime sax soloing from Wood and a great sax/piano duel from Wood and Lynne. There are also some great, typical Wood lyrics and overall this track has a wonderful stripped-back vibe, almost like the Beatles 'Get Back', hinting at that 'back to basics' sound that emulated the earlier days of rock and roll. Roy Wood would revisit this tone in his own, inimitable style with Wizzard further down the line, and overall it does sound like the band are enjoying themselves by letting off steam in the studio.

'No Time' (Lynne)

This is a gentle, acoustic ballad from Lynne, channelling the spirit of The Idle Race. It is much closer to his early songwriting style, taking the 'less is more' ethos to a higher level. If you listen to the lyrics, it's hardly cheery, contrasting a beautiful tune and with slightly darker lyrics. The song features a similar piano style to his bombastic 'Open Up (Said the World at the Door)' but is deployed in a much gentler fashion, reminiscent of the Beatles at their softest. Jeff's love of the Beatles is well known. He eventually produced them and worked with George, Ringo and Paul much later in their careers. While there's the feeling of homage about this song, it's not a Beatles rip off, but it borrows some familiar sounds, then channels them through Jeff's unique songwriting filter. Alongside some fine guitar work, it's also interesting how much of Jeff's songs are piano-driven – just listen to his work on this track for a start. His keyboard skills are utilised to their fullest on this album, more so than at any other point in his career.

'Don't Mess Me Up' (Bevan)
This 1950s-inspired rocker is the only songwriting credit on any Move or ELO album for drummer Bev Bevan, whose role in the story of The Move and ELO is sometimes understated. He was, after all, the only member of the group to stick with Roy Wood from the start and despite his initial reservations about the ELO project, he and Jeff Lynne were the only consistent members of the group from its inception till the original finish of the band in 1986.

Not only that, but he has drummed for Black Sabbath amongst others, so he should be regarded as one of the great drummers in the business. As for his songwriting, well, the jury is out. However, this is a splendid slice of rockabilly. Roy Wood gets to impersonate Elvis with a rollicking vocal – a style that he would later embrace more fully within Wizzard – and once again, this song is very much in keeping with the time, in that the overblown psychedelic sound had been pared down. Some of the artists at the turn of the decade were starting to revisit the acts that had inspired them, as the Beatles did with their *Get Back/Let it Be* project, an attempt to turn the clock back to more carefree days. This inspired a lot of other artists, and it's that kind of freewheeling approach to songwriting that makes this album so enjoyable. Roy gives it his all with, as the sleeve notes put it, a 'detectable midlands accent' and Jeff and Bev have some real fun with the doo-wop backing vocals. The 2005 remaster gives us another version of this as a bonus track, which strips back the instrumentation, emphasising the fabulous vocals. It sounds like great fun.

The instrumentation is minimal anyway, with some great shuffling drum fills from Bevan and some wonderful Chucky Berry-style guitar running through the track, not to mention a Jerry Lee Lewis-style piano solo from Jeff. This 'less is more' approach is evident throughout this album, and this is a fantastic pastiche that shows the variety of influences brought to the band by their members. Bev is credited as 'Bullfrog' on here, due to his trademark deep vocals, which were also utilised to great effect on The Move's debut album, and the joie de vivre of this song sums up how much fun this album is as a whole.

'Until Your Moma's Gone' (Wood)
This is another Wood rocker and another track on the album that could easily have been a single. Given that they were working on two full-length albums

– this and the first ELO record – and released a hat full of singles at the same time, all these songs amount to an immense burst of creativity equal only probably to George Harrison's *All things Must Pass*, recorded around the same time. The song has some funky, driving bass, and a vocal from Wood straight from 'Brontosaurus', not to mention loads of sax, and some sterling piano work from Jeff. This is a powerful, rocking track, propelled by that pounding bass funk sound of Wood, with a different, heavier tone to it, and great guitar solos from both Lynne and Wood, working well together.

Had this been on *Looking On*, the song would have been at least ten minutes long, with every instrument taking an extended solo and the guitars duelling. Here, the different approach reigns in all these different elements to create a powerful, concise, high-impact rock track clocking in at just over five minutes. Listening to the complexity and power of this song makes me wonder why I thought *Message* was such a slight album on first listen. It is perhaps because I had absorbed *Looking on*, and indeed the debut ELO album, in so much obsessive detail, loving the dense, English equivalent of the 'wall of sound' and the sheer madness exhibited in the songwriting, that when it came to *Message*, with its shorter songs – only The Moves debut album has more tracks on it – I was still looking for those progressive textures. In reality, there are more ideas across this album than some artists manage in an entire career, and while such a diverse approach doesn't necessarily suit everyone, it shows how versatile Lynne and Wood could be.

'It Wasn't My Idea To Dance' (Wood)

Kicking off side two, with a heavy guitar and woodwind riff, this is the nod to the psychedelia that had made Wood his name. It has some interesting and obscure lyrics that seem to suggest a tryst gone wrong, including 'It's too late to want your freedom, it wasn't my idea to dance'. This is a potent, dark piece of music, with the woodwind echoing round like carrion circling an ever-darkening sky, waiting to pounce on a weary traveller.

There's an air of controlled aggression within this song, as it builds and grows, the flip side to the optimism and joy of 'Flowers in the Rain'. Indeed, this could be a postcard from 'Cherry Blossom Clinic', the music is barely in control as it builds towards the finale, with discordant oboes and other woodwind dominating the final passage. This track manages to merge the sound of *Shazam* with that of *Looking On* and creates one of the more powerful tracks on the album. It's meaning may be elusive, but it is one of the most intriguing late-era Move songs, and definitely one of Wood's later Move masterpieces, on a very strong second side.

'The Minister' (Lynne)

This is a riff-driven and powerful Lynne rocker about the mysterious 'Minister' and is the only track on this album that sounds like it could have slotted straight onto the ELO debut without too much alteration. It is a cautionary tale about a sinister cleric, a con man preacher not unlike those fake prophets in the USA. Again, it's one of Lynne's observational songs, with a wonderfully complex riff, building, as the chorus fades, into a climactic and dense finale. While the previous two songs featured a sole Wood vocal, this brings the harmonies back to the fore, alongside some thumping bass from Wood. The only fundamental difference between this and ELO is the lack of traditional string instruments, so what sounds like a dense, string-driven finale, is in fact built together using multi-tracked guitars, and that makes it even more impressive. Woodwind – also used on the ELO album – is again a dominating factor, creating a dense instrumental fade out, which, much like the previous track, threatens to get out of control. There are elements here that will be familiar to anyone who has heard the closing section of '10538 Overture'. This is another of the album's masterpieces, and closer to ELO in style than anything else on the album.

'Ben Crawley Steel Company' (Wood)

Before the album's finest song, we get some light relief with a Bevan vocal, his second on a Move album after 'Zing Went The Strings Of My Heart' on the debut. This is another pastiche, this time of Johnny Cash – a country and western story about work, life and betrayal. Our protagonist goes to work at the Ben Crawley Steel Company, lamenting the time away from his good lady, and in the tradition of the all the best country songs, he ends up burning down the company – a line delivered with relish and glee by Bevan, who really sounds like he's throwing himself into the role – because its manager has been sleeping with his wife while he's been slaving away at work. It's a simplistic country tale, and its instrumentation is appropriate, specifically Wood's steel guitar, with some nice harmony vocals from Lynne and Wood. The song feels like the equivalent of Ringo's contributions to Beatles albums, in that it is slight but entertaining enough. However, in the context of this album, and due to the intensity of the three songs that preceded it, this track acts as light relief, balancing the album and helping get that mix of light and dark just right. The art of programming a great album is one that seems to be getting lost in this day of downloads. It is a real shame because albums like this were designed and programmed by their creators to be listened to in a specific order. Yes, this might be a tongue in cheek Johnny Cash homage, and no, it doesn't have the depth of 'It Wasn't My Idea To Dance', but it's still fun, and it shows how relaxed the band were during the recording of this album. Placing it where it sits on side two, was a masterstroke, as it paves the way for the next song, this album's stand out track.

'The Words Of Aaron' (Lynne)

This is a Lynne masterpiece and one of his finest tracks for The Move. Like most of his songs on this album, it's piano-driven, but blends with other keyboards (particularly synth) and some pounding bass from Roy. The blend of their voices is particularly effective here, with Wood's harmony vocals slightly higher; it's sublime stuff. The song is reminiscent of 'Open Up Said The World At The Door' from *Looking On*, with mythical overtones, addressing lyrical themes Lynne would return to later – 'look at the dancing girls, see them holding hands across the world' – a blend of the ordinary with the mystical. Lynne Casts himself as an observer, watching the world, placing himself in the third person, a technique Jeff would go on to use with ELO. The climax of the song combines piano with flute in astonishing fashion – this is music that eats into your soul. 'The Words of Aaron' was the only track that I appreciated the first time I heard *Message From The Country*, and while other tracks reveal their majesty to the listener with repeated plays, this track grabbed me from the start. The track finishes with a big fade out, which is revealed to be a false ending, as the drums power back up for a few moments more.

The Move is seen, by music historians, as the place that Lynne did his apprenticeship, and that in ELO he became the songwriter that he is revered as today. It is clear, however, that when Lynne joined The Move, he was already an accomplished composer. What The Move did with Lynne was push him on. With a friend and competitor in the hugely talented Roy Wood, Jeff had no choice but to up his game, resulting in the most accomplished albums by the band. There is little doubt that some of the tracks here are bona fide classics, the only shame being that bar 'Do Ya', he hasn't re-recorded any of his other Move songs. Discovering these songs for the first time, make it possible to hear how he honed that ELO sound and how he used The Move to experiment with different studio techniques that would pay dividends as his career developed. On the 2005 re-master, there is an outtake of this song, which shows how it developed and how skilful Roy and Jeff were in the studio.

'My Marge' (Wood and Lynne)
This is not a celebration of a butter substitute, but instead, this is *Message from the Country's* equivalent of the 'Duke of Edinburgh's Lettuce'. Again, it's a piece of fun from Wood and Lynne, both of whom loved Musical Hall comedy. The bouncing piano and the heavily mannered vocals provide a charming pastiche of songs from the era (which would be celebrated on TV later in the 1970s in *the Good Old Days*) and, again, it is very knowing of the band. Rather than finish on some big epic, they decide to close the album in an upbeat mood, a nod to similar efforts by the Beatles (songs like 'Your Mother Should Know' and 'When I'm 64' spring to mind). However, it is ironic that the last musical statement on an album by The Move would be a slight ditty about a woman called Marge. Perhaps that's what the band intended, and it rounds off their finest and most well-rounded collection of tracks.

Looking On and *Message From The Country* are both albums that I return to on a regular basis. There is little doubt that The Move, when led by Roy Wood and Jeff Lynne, was the most impressive era of the band. A DVD release by Gonzo multimedia – sadly unavailable now, but still available on Youtube

– features German Broadcasts of The Move augmented by Bill Hunt (later of Wizzard) on piano and Richard Tandy (who later joined ELO) on bass. They rattle through some of the classics, including a blinding version of 'Words of Aaron' which has Lynne and Hunt duelling on piano. It's a stunning version of this song, complete with Wood in a crazy, proto-glam yellow suit.

These are some of my favourite albums of all time and remain as important to me as they were when I first listened to them.

The Final Singles

After the *Message From the Country,* The Move bowed out in style with a trio of top thirty singles, which kept the band in the public eye and on *Top of the Pops*, ensuring that the band ended gracefully rather than just fading away on the back of an under-appreciated album.

'Tonight' b/w 'Don't Mess Me Up' (Wood)

Harvest release 21 May 1971
Personnel:
Roy Wood: vocals, oboe, guitar, steel guitar, bass, clarinet, bassoon and all saxes.
Jeff Lynne: vocals, piano, guitars, electric piano and percussion
Bev Bevan: drums, percussion and vocals
Produced by Roy Wood and Jeff Lynne
Highest UK Chart position:11
'Tonight' is available on: *Magnetic Waves of Sound: The Best of The Move,* Esoteric, 2017
'Don't Mess Me Up' is available on *Message From The Country*.

It's such a shame that the re-mastered version of *Message* is no longer available except via streaming services, as these singles were all included as bonus tracks and provided a complete chronological record of the entire output of The Move on CD. 'Tonight', is a very different kind of track; an acoustically-driven Wood song, with some wonderful lyrics, and great vocal sparring between Wood and Lynne. Running underneath the piece are some wonderful slide and electric guitars, and while it seems like a simple tune, there's a great deal going on musically, with some wonderful, funky bass and some great rock vocals. One of the lesser-known Move tunes, this love song is one of my favourite singles by the band. On release, it hovered outside the top ten. There was still life in the old band yet.

'Chinatown' (Wood) / 'Down On The Bay' (Lynne)

Harvest release 1 October 1971
Highest Chart position in the UK: 23
Personnel:
Roy Wood: vocals, oboe, guitar, steel guitar, bass, clarinet, bassoon and all saxes.
Jeff Lynne: vocals, piano, guitars, electric piano and percussion

Bev Bevan: drums, percussion and vocals
Produced by Roy Wood and Jeff Lynne
'Chinatown' is available on *Magnetic Waves of Sound: The Best of The Move.*
'Down on the Bay' is not currently available

The follow up to 'Tonight', 'Chinatown', lacks the most politically correct lyrics, but attempts an evocation of Birmingham's Chinatown area, with some wonderful slide guitar and, once again, a pared-back arrangement. It is acoustically driven with some fantastic harmony vocals from Wood and Lynne, in what is very much a dual vocal approach. Wood's lyrics are again evocative of a lover's tryst and the excitement of a lad from Birmingham heading into Chinatown for the night. It is a straightforward folk-rock song, with pseudo oriental sounds scattering through the tune. As was a trademark of The Move in this final era, the vocals of Wood and Lynne bounce off each other, in a to and fro style not dissimilar to the early work of Lennon and McCartney. These early 1970s singles defined The Move 'sound', in contrast to the big bombastic textures that Lynne, Wood and Bevan would unleash with the ELO project.

'Down on the Bay'. Like so many of the songs on both *Message From The Country* and this last batch of singles, the defining influences for Lynne and Wood at this point were late 1950s / early 1960s rock and roll, a sound that both writers would return to. Wood moved to that style with Wizzard a lot sooner than Lynne, but even he had had some great rock and roll-influenced songs in late period ELO (See 'Don't Bring Me Down', 'Hold on Tight', and 'Rock and Roll Is King') not to mention his *Long Wave* album of recordings of music he grew up with.

This evocation of the Rock 'n' Roll era permeated the whole glam scene in the UK, with artists like Alvin Stardust, Mud, Sweet and the now shamed Gary Glitter, who all who brought a touch of colour back to *Top of the Pops* on the BBC. With its faux Americana and pared-back lyrics and arrangement, this is the sound of a band having fun. A dirty Chuck Berry-esque riff kicks the song off, with some great fuzz guitar work and a nice guitar counter-melody to Lynne's mid-western (as opposed to West Midland) vocals. The solo has a dirty rock and roll sound to it and alongside the sing-a-long lyrics, it has a jiving bassline reminiscent of an Elvis tune, bringing the song to a big finish with some wild duck quacking. Considering its B-side status, this isn't a throwaway track. To create something as accessible and funky as this, complete with its faux Elvis mumbling as the song ends, takes some real skill. And there's not a single violin in sight. It is just a shame it's not currently available on any physical release.

'California Man' (Wood) / **'Do Ya'** (Lynne) / **'Ella James'** (Wood)
Harvest release 14 April 1972
Personnel:
Roy Wood: vocals, oboe, guitar, steel guitar, bass, clarinet, bassoon and all saxes.

Jeff Lynne: vocals, piano, guitars, electric piano and percussion
Bev Bevan: Drums, percussion and vocals
Produced by Roy Wood and Jeff Lynne
Highest UK chart position: 7
'California Man' & 'Do Ya' are available on: ***Magnetic Waves of Sound: The Best of The Move***
'Ella James' is on ***Message from the Country***
Parlophone/Warner Brothers 2014

The Move had been in a state of managed decline, as the band and label were gearing up for the transformation to The Electric Light Orchestra. 'California Man' is another one those rock and roll pastiches that were Wood and Lynne's stock trade at this point. This three-track maxi-single was The Moves last gasp and showed them going out in real style. The two new tracks on here ('California Man' & 'Do Ya') show the different routes that Wood and Lynne would head in with Wizzard and ELO, with both tracks influencing the two men further down the line than maybe either anticipated at this point. Influenced by Jerry Lee Lewis and with some top-notch piano playing in Lewis' style by Jeff, he and Roy share the vocals. Jeff, in particular, puts on a fantastic rock and roll voice, borrowing vocal ticks from both Elvis and Roy Orbison, while Roy Wood's manic sax duels with Jeff's piano. It all feels wonderfully authentic – full-on rock and roll from the early 1970s – channelling the original spirit of rock from the 1950s complete with a shouted 'take it Jeffery' from Roy as the piano solo kicks in.

These last few years were kind to The Move, as the two band leaders had a specific vision for what they wanted to do with the group and they drew a distinct line between where they were going with ELO, and what they wanted to achieve with The Move. This last blast of powerful rock singles (complete with more of Wood's saxes – to become a feature of Wizzard) was as strong a run of hits as the band had ever had. Free of internal disputes and arguments about the direction, meant that their legacy was left intact with a sterling last album, and these final, magnificent singles. 'California man' is not only sheer fun, but it also respects the genre to which it is paying homage. Less than two months after this was released, The Move were gone, and the next time we saw Lynne, Wood and Bevan on *Top of the Pops* it was as The Electric Light Orchestra, with the vastly different '10538 Overture'.

'Do Ya'. For those of you familiar with the work of ELO you will recognise this as the penultimate track on their 1976 album *A New World Record*. Here is the original version. It's another of Jeff's rockers, with some great vocals, some wonderful slide guitar, and, in what would become a bit of a Lynne trademark, a contemplative middle section before the riff kicks back in. Once again, the song has some powerful harmonies, some great rock and roll vocals from Jeff, and call and response vocals with Roy Wood. This is, effectively, proto ELO (sans violins) at its finest. Indeed, play this alongside 'Mamma Belle' or

'Showdown', and you can tell the DNA running through it. The song has a big, chunky, sing-along chorus and thumping drums from Bevan – a trick utilised to great effect by Lynne later in his career. That it the song was re-recorded by ELO says a great deal about the quality of it and while, as an ELO fan, I am used to the more polished and string driven version, I prefer this version, for it's raw, more animal edge. The guitar solos sound barely restrained; Wood's vocals are deliberately far less polished than those of the late Kelly Groucutt on the ELO version and with its ramshackle 'Look out baby, there's a plane a coming' (the working title of the song) and power trio aesthetic, it's a highly satisfying tune. It is odd though, after knowing it as part of *A New World Record* for the past twenty-odd years, not having 'Shangri-La' fading up after the track takes some getting used to.

'Do Ya' b/w 'No Time' (Lynne)

Harvest release 13 September 1974
Highest UK chart position: did not chart
Availability: Do Ya is on: *Magnetic Waves of Sound: The Best of The Move* Esoteric Records 'No time' is on *Message from the Country*
Currently only available in *Roy Wood The Original Album Series*

By 1974, when this version was reissued by Harvest, ELO had signed to Warner Bros and were highly successful in America. 'Do Ya' had made its way into the bands live set and so what else could a record label do, given that had the rights to the only recorded version by its composer, but reissue it? They reissued the single complete with a B-side from the *Message* album, hoping to cash in. Unfortunately for Harvest, the single didn't trouble the charts.

As a postscript to the 'Do Ya' story, the reason ELO re-recorded it for *New World Record*, was that Todd Rundgren's cover version was the best-known version of the song in the US, and Jeff wanted to reclaim the song as his own. It went on to be a hit for ELO in 1977 in the states reaching number 22 and was re-recorded yet again by Jeff Lynne for *Mr Blue Sky: The Very Best of Electric Light Orchestra* released in 2012, making it his only song by The Move to have survived the band's transition into The Electric Light Orchestra and its current incarnation, Jeff Lynne's ELO.

4. The Electric Light Orchestra

This book is not about Jeff Lynne and the Electric Light Orchestra. Indeed, the success the group had after Roy Wood left to form Wizzard in 1972 could – and has – filled other books. However, the first album, simply called *Electric Light Orchestra* in the UK (and *No Answer* in the States), was fundamental to that later success and also represented the last chapter in the story of The Move.

I first discovered ELO in the mid-1990s, through rifling through my parent's record collection, where I found the lush pop perfection of *Out of the Blue*. It was through second-hand vinyl and record fairs that I discovered the groups back catalogue. It was only on reading more about the group that it became apparent that Jeff Lynne had been in The Move and that Roy Wood had been in ELO. The formation of this band had been the catalyst Jeff needed to leave the Idle Race and join The Move, as the intention was to turn The Move into the Electric Light Orchestra project,and for pretty much all of 1971, the two bands co-existed in the studio and on the road, as the same core members, Jeff Lynne, Roy Wood and Bev Bevan were in both bands. Confusing?

While in 1971, The Move (as discussed earlier) had a run of late-period chart hits, The Electric Light Orchestra was funded by those singles, and found their character through many overdubs and experiments in the studio. This meant that there was a lot of sonic overlap between *Message From The Country* and *Electric Light Orchestra*. Indeed, compared to their pop heyday in the mid-70s, the first Electric Light Orchestra, seems a totally different beast – a million miles away from the polished sound of 'Turn to Stone' or 'Mr Blue Sky'. It feels far more medieval, ragged, darker and heavier.

As you peel away the layers and immerse yourself in this album, you see there is still the pop/rock sensibilities of The Move, but this is combined with – as both Jeff and Roy said – their desire to 'pick up where "I am the Walrus" left off'. It's the emphasis on the strings, woodwind and cellos that make this markedly different to any 'pop' music that had gone before. Indeed, the album is enhanced by the fact that Roy Wood is such a gifted musician that he could put his hands on any instrument and utilise it to create the sound he and Jeff Lynne were looking for.

As with both previous Move albums, this was a co-production between Roy and Jeff, and while the songwriting honours were split between them, there were no co-writes. However, this is a musical highpoint for both Lynne and Wood's careers, marking the culmination of their previous few years work towards changing musical direction away from The Move, and it is a shame that due to external pressures, Wood felt he had to move on to his own project, Wizzard. It would have been interesting to see what he and Jeff might have come up with next.

This remains a personal favourite amongst ELO albums and one that encapsulates all the freedom and experimentation that was rife in the early 1970s, where musicians were pushing boundaries in sounds and styles, not just because they wanted to, but because they could and because both the public and the record labels were willing for them to experiment and push themselves and their music, as far as they wanted. It's hard to imagine in these days of commercial pop, seeing a band like ELO – with Roy in proto- glam mode – performing '10538 Overture' on any of the major music TV shows, as they were able to do on the single's release in 1972.

The Electric Light Orchestra (album US title: No Answer)

Personnel:

Jeff Lynne: vocals, piano, electric guitar, acoustic guitar, percussion, bass, Moog synthesizer

Roy Wood: vocals, cello, classical acoustic guitar, bass, double bass, oboe, bassoon, clarinet, recorder, slide guitar, percussion, bass clarinet, crumhorn

Bev Bevan: drums, timpani, percussion

Bill Hunt: French horn, hunting horn, piccolo trumpet

Steve Woolam: Violin

Produced by Jeff Lynne and Roy Wood

Originally released on Harvest Records in the UK on 1 December 1971

Originally released on United Artists in the US in early 1972

Electric Light Orchestra (2001 remaster) available on EMI/Harvest Records

The Harvest Years 1970-1973 (2006) includes the 2001 remaster, the single edit of '10538 Overture', the second album *ELO2* and the rare 1973 Quad mix of *The Electric Light Orchestra*. EMI/Harvest Records

Roy Wood The Original Album Series. Parlophone/Warner Brothers 2014

Highest Chart Positions: UK: 32 US: 196

This album bears very little relation to the more polished synth and strings-driven pop that the Jeff Lynne fronted version of ELO brought to the fore, and rather more interesting than the Bev Bevan-driven ELO part II of the late 1980s & 1990s. The album takes Wood and Lynne's baroque and roll ethos to its logical conclusion and was recorded during the inevitable wind-down of The Move. It can be seen as a companion to the *Message From The Country* album, with various elements of their songwriting seeping between the two projects – and there are also certain elements in Roy Wood's songwriting here that filters through to the debut Wizzard album. Indeed, it's hard sometimes to guess where The Move stopped and ELO began. The reason why the American version of this iconic debut album had a different title, was because a record company executive at the US label asked his secretary to phone the UK to get the album title and as she couldn't get hold of anyone, she left a note on his desk on which she'd written the words 'No Answer'.

This album is the difference between steam power and electricity. It has a darker, rawer, rougher around the edges sound, with an intense, sinister, dark and otherworldly character to it. After multiple plays, it's still easy to hear bits that the listener has missed. The songs have multi-layered depth; riffs sneaks out and starts to build and the style is quirky, evoking structured chaos, pushing studio technology beyond where it could go at the time. It is an album of rare beauty and charm and ELO would never sound this ragged, raw or as exciting again. As with The Move, the ELO that made this album and *Out Of The Blue* are the same band in name alone.

There was never another ELO album like this one, although Jeff wrote within a similar style on *ELO 2* (1973). Roy only appears (uncredited at the time) on two tracks, 'In Old England Town' and 'From the Sun to the World' playing cello and bass and without the more experimental edge that Roy Wood brought to this debut album, you could tell the direction in which Jeff was going to take ELO, which he did with great success.

While this album is very much the odd one out in the ELO catalogue, when we see it in the context of the evolution of both The Move and the Idle Race, it is the culmination of five years work for both songwriters. Not only had it evolved logically from work they had done previously, taking the best parts of their songwriting skills and building something new around them, but it also acts as a signpost towards the different directions in which both men were heading: the more straightforward, well-crafted rock and strings of Jeff Lynne's ELO, against the more experimental and alternative approach to rock and roll that Roy Wood brought to bear with Wizzard and their mix of old school rock, blues, sax driven prog with even – eventually – hints of free form jazz.

Operating within the constraints of ELO and with Jeff Lynne, the band was never going to be big enough to contain all the musical ideas that Roy had. With The Move, the band initially began as a vehicle to perform Roy's songs, but by the time of the Electric Light Orchestra, Jeff Lynne – the apprentice – had overtaken the master and had a clear vision as to where he wanted to go. Roy's more eclectic and diverse ideas were far too big to fit into one single box, as can be discovered when we look into the work of Wizzard and his solo career in more depth.

The Electric Light Orchestra album is simultaneously the end of one era for Roy Wood – the days of The Move were well and truly over – and the start of a new chapter for both him and Jeff Lynne. This is where their two-year partnership, that helped create some of the most interesting and exciting albums of the early 1970s, as well as providing some great hit singles, came to it's natural end. This was never going to be a Lennon/McCartney-style partnership, and it was inevitable that both musicians would take different paths. Nonetheless, this remains a great album, combining a unique approach to making music with the intensity and depth of some of its performances – there is really no other album like it.

'10538 Overture' (Lynne)
Released as a single, **b/w 'First Movement (Jumping Biz)'**
Released on Harvest in the UK on 23 June 1972
United Artists in the US 29 July 1972
Currently available on *The Harvest Years 1970-1973* (2006) EMI/Harvest Records
Highest UK Chart position: 9

This is the albums lead track and was indeed its lead – and only – single in a form edited down for radio from the album-length of 5.32 to 4.04. It was originally destined as a Move B-side and has a similar chord structure to Lynne's 'The Minister' from *Message From The Country*. It became the starting point for the new ELO project, and as Wood said in the sleeve notes to the remastered album:

> After recording the basic backing track the other guys went home, leaving Jeff and myself to do the overdubs… I had just acquired this cheap Chinese cello… I sat in the control room trying out this cello and messing around with Jimi Hendrix type riffs. Jeff said 'That sounds great, why don't we throw it on the track' I ended up recording around 15 of these… it was beginning to sound like some monster heavy metal orchestra. In fact, it sounded just bloody marvellous.

It does sound 'bloody marvellous', indeed, Roy. It was nothing like anyone had ever heard before. It has a dark, ominous guitar riff (later borrowed by perennial rock magpie Paul Weller for his 'Changing Man' single) and sinister lyrics, with the '10538' of the title being an escaped prisoner. The call and reply nature of Lynne and Wood's vocals are perfect, and with the powerful, driving cello riffs mirroring the guitar work, and the crazy overdubbing, it makes this an incredibly powerful statement of intent. Lynne is obviously still fond of the track, as he re-recorded it in 2012 for his own album that reinterpreted tracks from the ELO canon, and it has appeared on recent ELO setlists.

'Look at Me Now' (Wood)
This opening song is a mix of baroque music, dark chamber orchestration and Roy Wood's eschewing of conventional musical instruments. The track is essentially a ballad about opening his heart. Instead of guitar solos, you have the sound of the crumhorn, violin and acoustic melodies, with the riffs played largely on the cello. This isn't just deconstructing the love song; this is taking a very simple idea, and building it into something brand new and unique.

'Nellie Takes Her Bow' (Lynne)
Nellie is another one of Jeff Lynne's musical characters, one of the loners and lost from the cast that inhabited *The Birthday Party*. However, instead of the pessimism, or the unknown, this is a complete narrative, relating the story of someone who wants to be somebody else and live her life as another person.

The difference between Lynne and Wood's compositions are more obvious when you play this back to back with 'Look At Me Now'. This track is cello driven and has a wonderfully intense middle section that cribs from 'God Rest Ye Merry Gentleman'. Lynne's writing and song-structuring is more guitar-driven, while Wood is thinking outside the guitar, and that's where the very best of their collaborative approaches worked. Lynne has a storytelling songwriter's heart, and puts plenty of soul into this track, where our heroine Nellie gets what she wants – a lead role on Broadway – and while the music has the same intensity and depth that typifies the album, this is not a million miles away either from Jeff's observational songs in latter-day ELO and early Idle Race. The song is given a lot of space and room to breathe, making it one of the most impressive songs on the album.

'The Battle of Marston Moor (July 2nd, 1644)' (Wood)

This is a very specific title, referring to a decisive battle in the English Civil War, even though another band called Cromwell had released a track with the same title on their eponymous concept album about the war. This track, however, is largely made up of medieval instruments and begins with a spoken word passage from Roy Wood decrying the King. At that point, musical chaos ensues, consisting of a very deep musical interpretation of the battle with instruments clashing, representing the opponents fighting. This is the most striking track on the album, and one totally at odds with the one it follows. Yet that contrast, the mix between Wood's more intense experimentation and Lynne's pop sensibilities, are what makes this album unique. Where else would you have songs about prisoners escaping, Broadway debuts and decisive English Civil War battles nestling alongside each other? And that's only on side one.

Easy listening this isn't, but progressive, in the truest sense of the word, it is. Wood goes to town here and free from the classic pop idioms, he can expand his soundscapes, show his prowess on the numerous instruments he has at his disposal and really let rip with some sublime and intricate musical invention.

'First Movement (Jumping Biz)' (Wood)

This track has a vibe of Mason William's Classical Gas. However, Roy's compositional skills and multi-instrumentalist talents bring this song to life. It's full of verve and a catchy riff as well, showing some of the difference between this initial ELO incarnation and some of the later ones, as woodwind and other wind instruments are very much to the fore, a tone that is markedly different from the string-driven incarnations of later line ups. In fact, this has elements of Roy's instrumental dexterity and prowess that would resurface in some of Wizzard's instrumental moments, showing the extent of his compositional skill as he moves further away from three-minute pop songs, to full-on baroque pieces.

'Mr Radio' (Lynne)

This is another one of Jeff's lonely character songs, in which a lonely listener whose wife has left him gets immersed in the world of the radio. The track is full of driving strings, matching the darker lyrical content with a more upbeat and up-tempo sound, a trick again used in The Idle Race. This could easily, with some slightly different arrangements, have come from *The Birthday Party*, with its gothic strings and piano work, which then jumps into chamber music and violin solos. It also suggests the direction in which Jeff's songwriting might be going. It also uses phased radio tuning effects as it crosses from one style to another to simulate the change of radio frequency and station. The couplet 'a weatherman has died, it makes me cry' harks back to the second Idle Race album. Has Jeff killed off the unknown weatherman?

'Manhattan Rumble (49th Street Massacre)' (Lynne)
The only Lynne instrumental on the album, this is quite a funky little shuffle, mixing up some traditional rock instrumentation and the classical vibe that runs throughout the record. It mixes traditional instrumentation and a little bit of jazz piano with some violin duelling.
Despite the presence of the cellos, this sounds very different to anything else on the album, being more piano-driven and with some great female scat vocals, it drives and builds. The little synth sections suggest passages in some later ELO instrumentals, as does the track in general.

'Queen Of The Hours' (Lynne)
This is yet another of Jeff's storytelling songs, with some folky violin and haunting vocals, plus plenty of that overdubbed cello in the background. Who is the Queen Of The Hours? The song has a very medieval feel to it, and again the haunting woodwind of Roy Wood adds a huge amount to this track. While this is very much a Lynne song, the collaborative production between the two of them is exciting. The way they skilfully blend the instrumentation to create a hybrid between rock, folk and classical music and something totally new is wonderful to behold. The violin of Steve Woolam provides a counterpoint to Jeff's vocals and gives this song it's hook, pulling the listener in, while the overdubs never get too heavy, but add depth to the sound.

'Whisper In The Night' (Wood)
This song is probably the most straightforward of Roy's on this album, and it's another plaintive ballad. With its strings and cello, it sounds more like the work on his solo album *Boulders* (more of that later) and is the first of his lovely, big, beautiful ballads, where the tenderness and his emotive vocals are matched by swelling musical orchestration. The overdubbed harmony vocals and the medieval instrumentation turn what could have been a very simple and throwaway song into something far more substantial. A darker musical interlude turns into the final verse, with soaring strings, a direct contrast to the darker sound of the cello. This is an exceptionally well-realised and executed ballad, with some of Roy's finest vocals on the album.

5. Wizzard and Roy Wood's Wizzo Band

For the purposes of continuity, I will be looking at the singles and the four albums that were an evolution of the Wizzard sound as one group, as the same musicians flowed through each line-up and the evolution of the sound was driven by the other members of Wizzard and The Wizzo Band as well as Roy.

Wizzard took Wood's rock and roll homage sound to new areas. From the proto-glam vibe of 'Brontosaurus' to the string of hit singles in the early 1970s, Wizzard were one of the defining bands of the Glam era, alongside fellow West Midlanders Slade and also T-Rex. However, like Slade and T-Rex, Wood and Wizzard were inextricably linked to the Glam scene and when they wanted to move on and expand their sound, they were never able to shake loose those chains.

Slade were only able to escape from that scene in the early 1980s, after a torrid late 1970s, while Marc Bolan tragically died in 1977 just as he was on the cusp of a return to the music scene. Wood's Wizzard evolved into the Wizzo Band before fading away entirely and are now almost only associated with the perennial Christmas song 'I Wish it Could Be Christmas Every Day'. This does them a massive disservice, as a listen to the albums they created have plenty of variation, as is always the case with anything that Roy has his hand in.

At the end of May 1972, The Move had their last chart hit and ELO hit the road. During some fraught sessions for the second ELO album, Roy ended up hooking up with former Move bassist Rick Price's band Mongrel, which then evolved into Wizzard. By June 1972 Roy had walked away from the Electric Light Orchestra entirely and launched Wizzard. Three top ten singles and a top 30 album indicated he'd made the right choice. However, in common with The Move for much of their existence, what Wizzard released on their singles was totally different from how their albums sounded. *Wizzard Brew*, until it's expanded remastering in 2006 brought together all the contemporaneous single A and B sides, is one of the craziest albums ever to escape during those fertile and febrile days of the early 1970s and anyone buying it on the strengths of the singles expecting more of the same, must have had their minds blown.

The Wizzard Singles

All songs produced by Roy Wood
Personnel:
Roy Wood: vocal, electric guitars, sitar, cello, bassoon, baritone saxophone, string bass, Bb Bass Tuba, trombone, recorders, percussion, euphonium and military drums
Rick Price: bass guitar, vocals and percussion
Bill Hunt: piano, harpsichord, French horn, trumpet, flugal horn, tenor horn, bugle, euphonium, Eb tuba and little glass trumpet, backing vocals.
Hugh 'H' McDowell: cello and Moog
Nick Pentelow: tenor saxophone, clarinet and flute, bass backing vocals

Mike Burney: alto, tenor baritone and synthesised saxes, clarinets and flute
Keith Smart: drums
Charlie Grima: drums, congas, percussion

'Ball Park Incident' (Wood) b/w 'The Carlsberg Special (Pianos demolished, phone 021 373 4472)' (Hunt)

Released December 1972 on Harvest
Highest UK Chart Position: 6
'Ball Park Incident' currently available on *Roy The Wizzard – Greatest Hits and More*
Harvest/Parlophone, released 2006
'The Carlsberg Special' is available to download and stream

From 'California Man', '10538 Overture' and then to 'Ball Park Incident', Roy Wood hit the singles charts in 1972 with three different bands and three very different sounds. I don't think anyone else has ever managed this in one year, and it shows the complete breadth and scope of his vision as a songwriter.
He was taking a totally different musical path to that of his former bandmates in the Electric Light Orchestra. In the notes to the *Wizzard Brew* remaster, a contemporary interview quotes Roy as saying that he quit ELO 'while Jeff and I were still friends', and it's testimony to his vision that within weeks he had formed a new band.

Taking as a jumping-off point, the rock and roll homages that he had been writing in The Move, 'Ball Park Incident' is chock full of American 1950's rock and roll images. From the lyrics 'sitting in the Ball Park on the North West side of town,' a funky riff is driven by saxophones and Bill Hunt's piano, giving the song a feel that is part Jerry Lee Lewis, part Elvis part Beach Boys. The Incident itself is all about someone shooting his baby at the 'ball park out of school', and like all the best stories, what it doesn't tell, is just as intriguing as what it does.

The flipside: Starting a tradition that carried through the Wizzard days, Roy put on the B-side songs written by other members of the band to ensure they got royalties and, as he also did with his own singles, plenty of instrumentals. This is written by pianist and arranger Bill Hunt, who had also guested with The Move on some German TV broadcasts and is a driven by his barrelhouse piano style. He was an excellent pianist and great musical foil to Wood. It's also the closest to The Move/ELO sound that Wizzard ever got, as it mixes classical instrumentation and Roy's trademark sitar solo's with added sax and that big beat from the double drummers, which were such an integral part of Wizzard's Sturm und Drang. It really works, and like many of the B-sides, it allowed relatively unsung members of the band to show their talents.

'See My Baby Jive' (Wood) b/w 'Bend Over Beethoven (The official follow up to 'California Man')' (Hugh McDowell)

Released April 1973 on Harvest
Highest UK Chart position: 1

'See my Baby Jive' currently available on *Roy The Wizzard- Greatest Hits and More*
Harvest/Parlophone, released 2006
'Bend Over Beethoven' is available to download and stream and is on the EMI
remaster

Roy's First number one with Wizzard, takes the classic rock and roll sound and
expands on it. A logical follow up to the debut single, it carries on the themes
and sounds from the first single but gives it a lot more oomph to it and it's
a far more energetic musical workout than 'Ballpark Incident'. The call and
answer chorus, and the emphasis on the sax, sees Roy taking his Midlands
wall of sound much further than that achieved by Phil Spector and in doing
so, put a lot of fun back into the charts. His mastery of the three-minute pop
song is here for all to see and again is one of the reasons why Roy should be
considered one of the finest songwriters the UK has produced.

The track also shows the contrast between the album and single versions of
the band. Here they tighten up their sound and bring everything to the party
over a three-minute mini-epic, while on the album they have room to expand
their sound and let it grow. The run of the first four Wizzard singles, two of
which were number ones and all of which were top ten hits, is an impressive
one and at complete odds with their album sound, returning again to that
album vs singles conundrum that The Move suffered.

The flipside sees the cellist for both the Electric Light Orchestra and Wizzard
Hugh McDowell take centre stage with his own composition. The title is a very
cheeky nod towards the band that he left (and then returned to) who were
currently strolling through the charts with their string-driven version of 'Roll
Over Beethoven'. With some funky bass and Bill Hunt's piano, this gets a really
low grove going and is far jazzier than its A-side would suggest. It carries on
the tradition of putting an instrumental on the back of the single. Indeed, the
funky time change and sax breaks make this closer to what some of the more
eclectic progressive/jazz bands were doing and a direction which the band
expanded on in their debut album, as well as indicating where the band's
ultimate destination lay.

'Angel Fingers (A Teen Ballad)' (Wood) b/w 'You Got The Jump On Me' (Rick Price)

Released August 1973 on Harvest
currently available on *Roy The Wizzard- Greatest Hits and More*
Harvest/Parlophone, released 2006
Highest UK Chart position: 1
'You got the Jump on Me' is available to download and stream and is on the EMI
remaster

The A-side has more wailing sax, a big Motown production sound, lush
harmonies and Wood in full on balladeer mode. The song again mixes US

nostalgia with British traditions, as Roy sings about taking his motorbike down to 'that old café', which is reminiscent of the mods and rockers days out on their motorbikes or scooters, as they hit the seaside towns in the late 1950s and early 1960s. This condenses trademark 'sha la la' vocals and the mighty Wizzard wall of sound into seven inches of black plastic. There is a huge amount happening in this arrangement, yet the skill of Wood's production is that it doesn't sound cluttered or too busy. You can clearly hear the trademark sax, the piano of Bill Hunt – as integral to the Wizzard sound as the sax – and the dynamic double drumming sound.

The B-side starts with a mighty drum beat and this Rick Price rocker unsurprisingly has some powerful bass and vocals reminiscent of Robert Plant or Black Sabbath. This is a hard and heavy track, with some great guitar work and it puts rock right at the heart of the band. Price himself is stellar, his bass anchoring everything down and the heavier sound shows that Wizzard were more than capable of rocking out. This is closer in spirit to *Looking On*, proving that Price was more than happy with the band moving in a heavier direction. There is some stellar piano work from Bill Hunt who really pulls no punches and the pared-down production makes this song a genuine lost classic.

Ever so briefly available on the *Wizzard Brew* remaster, which told the complete Wizzard story from 1973-1974, it's a shame that this extended rocker that winds down with an extended piano break by Bill Hunt, clocks in at well over six minutes. It's worth hunting down to listen to a copy of this online.

'I Wish It Could Be Christmas Everyday' (Wood) b/w 'Rob Roy's Nightmare (A Bit More HA) (Mike Burney)

Released December 1973 on Harvest
UK Chart place: 4
'I Wish it Could Be Christmas Everyday' currently available on *Roy The Wizzard-Greatest Hits and More*
Harvest/Parlophone released 2006
'Rob Roy's Nightmare' is available to download and stream and is on the EMI remaster

This song is a perennial favourite in the UK and one of the big hitters of the classic Christmas songs. As a result, its ubiquity takes away some of its shine and even though Roy had had all those hits with The Move, for many people, this is the song they think of when they hear the name Roy Wood. The British know it's Christmas when Roy starts singing 'Let the bells ring out for Christmas' and his fellow Midlander Noddy Holder shouts 'It's Christmas'. That early 1970s era was the golden age of Christmas songs and nothing has been written since to top them.

The infectiousness of the tune, the production, the cash register at the start (a cheeky nod to the commercialisation of Christmas) and the sax sound, are all important features of the classic Christmas song and the crowning glory is the children's choir. British fans will remember Roy prancing around the stage in the *Top Of The Pops* performances with his beard dyed white and fake snow, making this is as traditional for Christmas as turkey, Brussel sprouts and new socks.

Continuing the tradition of instrumental B-sides, the flipside is a jazz-infused number, complete with sitar work out by Roy and instrumental breaks from the saxes. The track was written by sax man Mike Burney and it's a funky, mood-shifting little number, again indicates the direction of travel that Wizzard would take in later years.

Wizzard Brew (album)

All tracks composed and produced by Roy Wood
Personnel:
Roy Wood: vocal, electric guitars, sitar, cello, bassoon, baritone saxophone, string bass, Bb bass tuba, trombone, recorders, percussion, euphonium and military drums
Rick Price: bass guitar, vocals and percussion
Bill Hunt: piano, harpsichord, French horn, trumpet, flugal horn, tenor horn, bugle, euphonium, Eb tuba and little glass trumpet, backing vocals.
Hugh 'H' McDowell: cello and Moog
Nick Pentelow: tenor saxophone, clarinet and flute, bass backing vocals
Mike Burney: alto, tenor baritone and synthesised saxes, clarinets and flute
Keith Smart: drums
Charlie Grima: drums, congas, percussion
String arrangements by Roy Wood
Brass arrangements by Roy Wood and Bill Hunt
Engineered by Peter Oliff (Phonogram) and Alan Parsons (EMI)
Originally released on Harvest Records SHSP4025
UK May 1973
Highest UK Chart position: 29
Availability on EMI on the 2006 remaster with bonus tracks and as part of the *Roy Wood The Original Album Series*
Parlophone/Warner Brothers 2014

This is one hell of a record. In the late 1990s, to celebrate 30 years of the Harvest label, EMI reissued 'vanilla' versions of some of the labels bigger records. This edition of *Wizzard Brew*, with no bonus tracks and just an inner sleeve, was the first time it had been on CD. The cover depicts Roy as the archetypal Wizzard, mixing in the elements of the band into a cauldron as he creates sonic alchemy, and it is a perfect visual representation of this album. It sounds like nothing I'd heard before. I was very surprised to realise that a) none of the singles were on the album, b) there were only six tracks on it and c) three of them were over six minutes in length. This wasn't the cuddly glam rock look of the Wizzard that appeared on *Top Of The Pops*. This was intense, all-out proto-prog, and the album is more like *Looking On* than anything ELO were doing. It is an intense and powerful audio experience.

Wizzard Brew is an explosion of musical colour from a band that no-one, not least Roy Wood, was expecting him to be fronting when 1972 started. In less than twelve months, he had wound down The Move with a string of rock 'n roll inspired singles, helped launch the good ship ELO, which continues to sail to this day, and then created an album that is progressive in the truest sense of the word. 1973 was an amazing year for rock music, and yet *Wizzard's Brew* remains one of the years finest – and largely unsung – albums. It's a shame the expanded edition which covers all the 1972/73 singles and B-sides is no longer available, as playing the singles after the album shows how different and versatile the band could be.

'You Can Dance Your Rock 'n' Roll'
Opening with the dual drum kick of Smart and Grima, this opener is a percussive beast that propels along a song that starts off as the bastard cousin of 'Brontosaurus', while the massed brass section, mixed with overdubbed cellos, drift the music far beyond where Roy was contemplating going with ELO. This takes the wall of sound approach and ups the ante with some fantastically frantic playing, as the band builds and grooves on the riff, Roy utilising his best voice, before a sneaky 'Marston Moor' cello break arrives. This massed sound is Roy taking the widescreen approach to songwriting that he used with ELO and the reliance on overdubs, but instead of just using cellos, he now used the brass section to flesh out the sound and give it some real depth. There's a huge amount going on, so it's possible to find new things in the track every time you listen. As a statement of intent, and an opening shot on an album, it's big, brash, bold and brilliant.

'Meet Me At The Jailhouse'
A big, crunchy riff opens this epic thirteen minutes of intense power. We get some frantic and intense sax solos, before that riff hits back in at the two-minute mark. That's where the vocals start, and the piece really starts to groove. The two-drummer approach is spectacular and the way the song hits a real rhythm and allows the band to build around it is sublime.
The band grind out an intense metronomic beat, as the saxes and guitars solo, from speaker to speaker, using the stereo to full effect. Indeed, the main riff and the soloing are positively metal in their intensity, again more reminiscent of fellow Brummies' Black Sabbath. There does seem to be a guitar sound forged in the Midlands, and combined with the pounding drums, it recalls the old heavy industries and the heavy metal they used to shape into cars. Birmingham even gets name-checked in the verses.

The melodic counterpoint of the brass and the drums, bass and guitar all help build this track up as they hit real funk in the chorus. This is the equivalent of *Looking On* but on steroids, Roy taking the long-form experimentation of that song and pulling in far wider instrumentation. There an improvisational aspect to parts of this song that could easily be by Colosseum or Graham Bond's band and that heady mix of rock, jazz and powerful driving beats is something that Roy would take further in the future.

Around the ten minute mark, there is some mighty guitar sparring worthy of Wishbone Ash and the guitar suddenly launches into snippets of 'Jerusalem', while the beat pounds on, before an almighty sax onslaught and the tempo whirls and flies with shamanic intensity. This is a heady brew alright, and this track packs more ideas into its thirteen minutes than some bands do in their entire career. Indeed, for people expecting another 'Angel Fingers', this 'melt your face off' musical onslaught probably freaked them out, and maybe even scared them a little. It's spine-tingling stuff and feels way shorter than its thirteen minutes.

'Jolly Cup Of Tea'

After the swirling dervish that is 'Meet Me At The Jailhouse', we then get a military band march, massed vocals, and some proper 'oompah'-style sounds. This piece recreates the sound of the army marching bands as seen on many a parade, complete with the sing-along, chanted vocals in a very English style. In fact, this is a faux war song, similar in intent to 'It's A Long Way To Tipperary'. While it's the shortest song on the album, it does act as light relief from the madness of 'Jailhouse' and is still one of the strangest about turns in music on any album.

'Buffalo Station – Get On Down To Memphis'

This is another powerful, rocking track and a travelogue to the American rock and roll dream. Roy's vocals are incredibly intense again, putting his 'Californian Man' vocal-style to good effect. Roy taps into his love of Americana and the intensity of the band is like listening to tracks like 'See my Baby Jive', but with the brakes off. The band, here, is given full rein to play and you get a sense of barely controlled enthusiasm, as Roy's wonderful psych solo, with the cello of Hugh and piano of Bill Hunt, pull together a wonderfully sublime instrumental section.

Roy sings of a relationship with an American girl from the mid-west, and you get a real sense of big, fast cars and the wide-open spaces. Then you get a pounding, driving segue, with great interplay between the brass and drums, that leads into the second part of the track, the homage to Elvis in 'Get on down to Memphis', with some great vocals again from Roy. There's some wonderful Dixieland-style jazz interspersed with those pounding dual drums, the powerhouse behind the whole album. Roy dusts off his old Elvis impersonation, and there's some wonderfully Sun Studio style rockabilly piano from Bill, which keep this track motoring along. This is 'California Man' pumped up. If that song were a teenager, it'd be the equivalent of your gran not seeing you for six months and coming in and saying 'my, haven't you grown?'

'Gotta Crush About You'

More rollicking piano and some fantastic 'big band' sax kicks off this vibrant rocker. There are more rock and roll vocals from Roy and the track mixes the sort of American post-war big band swing sounds, with some pure Memphis Elvis as Roy sings about his girl. This song is really pared down compared to the other tracks on the album and the wall of sound here is reduced slightly. However, it still sees Roy pushing his songwriting out of the slightly restrictive constraints of The Electric Light Orchestra. You could say that with the different moods, themes and styles shown here on Wizzard, not only had Roy taken out the dressing up box for the outlandish stage items, he'd also opened the musical toy box and was playing around with every sort of sound and style he felt like using.

In fact, you could go so far to call Wizzard an Eclectic Light Orchestra.

'Wear A Fast Gun'

This is the second-longest song on the album and it continues a tradition of finishing the albums off with big epics – one that had started with 'Feel Too Good' on *Looking On*. This is a slower-paced, big ballad. Roy switches from rocker to full-on balladeer, with the band pulling no punches behind him, as the piccolo soars in the chorus. The heavily orchestrated backing, the powerful drums and the multi-faceted band playing their hearts out, give the listener the impression that this is the sound that Roy had been searching for with The Move and ELO. It combines many of his songwriting styles: the epic yearning ballad; the storytelling; the big widescreen sound and musical complexity and intensity.

Three minutes in, the pace becomes almost funereal, with the strings and brass beautifully rendered and some wonderfully moving vocals of Roy. He is widely praised, and rightly so, as a powerful songwriter, but he is also an incredibly effective vocalist, and here, as the front man of the band, this is the flowering of his musical visions, a culmination of his experiments with The Move. Movingly, the band sing the counter melody of 'Abide with Me' while Roy sings the chorus. As the piccolo soars, the sound drops. This is progressive music at its finest. Then Bill kicks in with a wonderful, classically-tinged piano before the strings return, an echo of the simplicity of 'Queen of the Hours', the beautifully scored melody creating a haunting interlude. Roy would return to scoring songs like this on albums like *Mustard* and *On the Road Again*. Underpinning it all, is the wonderfully mournful cello, played brilliantly by Hugh McDowell (who sadly passed away in 2018). Then the band returns with the choral ranks singing 'Abide with Me' and the track fades as the piccolo soars.

The Introducing Eddy And The Falcons Era

If 1973 was all about hit singles, then 1974 was all about a specific sound, and a culmination of a style of songwriting that Roy had pioneered made during the

Above: Despite not releasing any new material since 1985, Roy continues to tour. He's pictured on stage here sometime in the late 1990s. (*Gill Thomas @ Magic Arts*)

Left: The cover art for The Move's debut album was created by Dutch designers The Fool, who also worked on The Beatles' *Sgt. Pepper* album. (*Esoteric Recordings*)

Right: Previously out of print, the legendary *Something Else* EP brilliantly captures the early Move live experience. (*Esoteric Recordings*)

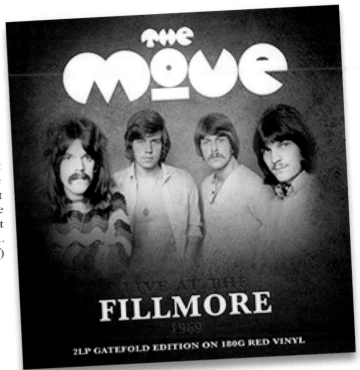

Right: Very few complete Move concerts exist, so this two-CD set showcasing the band's 1969 set was a welcome release when it came out in 2011. (*New Movement Ltd*)

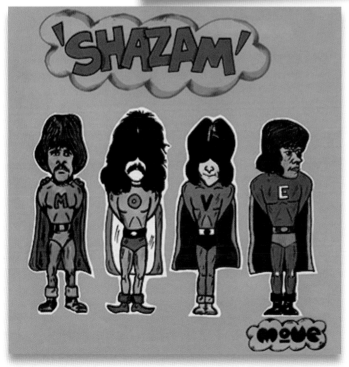

Left: The *Shazam* artwork was later revised for the 'Brontosaurus' single cover, the title hiding the fact that Carl Wayne had left the band. (*Esoteric Recordings*)

Left and below:
The Move's only UK number one in the UK, 'Blackberry Way' was demoed in Jeff Lynne's front room. Here we see it performed on *Colour Me Pop* in 1968.

Left: Despite the writing being on the wall for the Move with the release of the *Electric Light Orchestra* album, the band bowed out with a string of successful singles. Here we see them performing 'Tonight' in 1971.

Above and right: The Moves final single release saw the group bow out with yet another UK top ten hit. They are seen here performing 'California Man' on *Top Of The Pops*.

Left: *Looking On* was the first Move album to feature Jeff Lynne and showcases the change in direction that would lead to the Electric Light Orchestra. (*Esoteric Recordings*)

Right: *A Message To The Country*. The last Move album featured artwork by Roy Wood on the cover. (*Parlophone*)

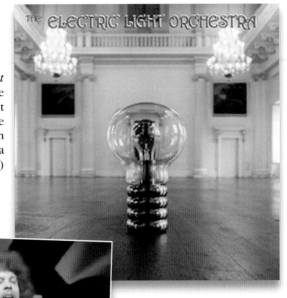

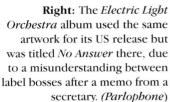

Right: The *Electric Light Orchestra* album used the same artwork for its US release but was titled *No Answer* there, due to a misunderstanding between label bosses after a memo from a secretary. *(Parlophone)*

Left and below: Developing a look devised from a TV performance by The Move, Roy's embryonic glam look would come to fruition when he launched Wizzard.

Left: 'See My Baby Jive'. When the critical acclaim for The Electric Light Orchestra failed to bring commercial rewards, Roy moved on and Wizzard saw Roy back in the top ten. *(Parlophone)*

Right: 'I Wish It Could Be Christmas Every Day'. This is the quintessential Christmas song, but due to contract confusion the promos were released by Warner Bros, although the actual single release was on the Harvest Label. *(Parlophone)*

Right: *The Wizzard Greatest Hits – The EMI Years*. Roy in full glam rock pose, a sight familiar to early 1970s *Top of the Pops* viewers. (*Parlophone*)

Left and below: Roy and the band in their full glam pomp. There was plenty of humour in their TV appearances. Here they are seen playing 'See My Baby Jive' on *Top Of The Pops*.

Left: The *Wizzard Brew* cover successfully depicts the musical alchemy at play throughout the album. (*Parlophone*)

Right: The contrast between the glam look and the rock 'n roll stylings of *Eddy And The Falcons* is most pronounced on its cover art. (*Esoteric Recordings*)

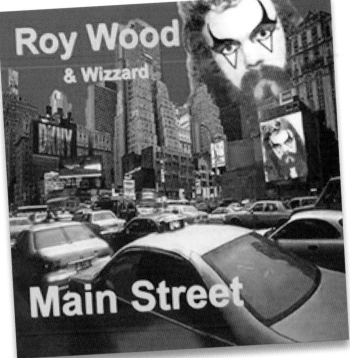

Right: The previously long-lost *Main Street* album. The music inside is better than its cover art. (*Esoteric Recordings*)

Left: Designed to look like a washing powder box, Roy is centre stage on the *Super-Active Wizzo* cover. (*Esoteric Recordings*)

BOULDERS

ROY WOOD

Left: *Boulders.* The drawing of Roy on this minimalistic cover is lifted straight from the *Message From The Country* artwork. (*Parlophone*)

Right: *Mustard* is another of Roy's own artworks. As well as the cover for this album, he also painted the illustration on the cover of Annie Haslam's *Annie In Wonderland.* (*Esoteric Recordings*)

Right: *On The Road Again*. Although the album was not released in the UK, ironically, the artwork features some traditional English countryside and parking meter! (*Parlophone*)

Left: Although the cover of *Starting Up* featured a bold new Samurai-inspired look for Roy, it appears that all expense was spared on the artwork itself. (*Sanctuary*)

Left: Throughout his recording career, Roy's longest musical association was with bassist Rick Price. Here they are performing 'Forever' on TV in 1973.

Right and below: Playing a Rock n Roll medley on the late-night TV show *OTT* in 1983. The band were Roy, Bev, Phil Lynott and Chaz Hodges.

Right: Back on EMI for the single 'Green Glass Windows', a lost classic. (*Parlophone*)

Left and below: Come Christmas, Roy pops up in all sorts of places with his perennial Yuletide classic. Here he is playing 'I Wish It Could Be Christmas Every Day' on *Christmas With The Kumars* in 2004.

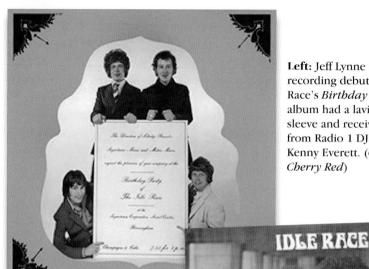

Left: Jeff Lynne made his recording debut with the Idle Race's *Birthday Party*. The album had a lavish gatefold sleeve and received much praise from Radio 1 DJs, including Kenny Everett. (*Grapefruit/ Cherry Red*)

Right: For the band's self-titled second album, there was no gatefold and an austere band picture. It seems that critical acclaim hadn't translated into commercial success. (*Parlophone*)

Left: *Time Is* was the last Idle Race studio album and the only record produced by the band after Jeff Lynne had joined The Move. The cover gives a rather literal demonstration of its title. (*Parlophone*)

last days of The Move. The title of *Introducing Eddy...* was either, depending on the sources, inspired by Frank Zappa's *Cruising With Ruben and the Jets* or the Beatles' *Sgt Peppers Lonely Hearts Club Band*, and the singles released by Wizzard that year are all influenced by Wood's love of old school rock and roll. As a result, instead of the freewheeling improvisational free for all that was *Wizzard Brew*, this was a much more controlled era for the band.

Wizzard were newly signed to Warner Brothers, and the album was released in a gatefold sleeve, depicting the table cloths of an old motorway café. The band toned down the previous years glam style, instead dressed up as a gang of rockers and the photos on the gatefold sleeve showing the photo session descending into a fight.

Again reminiscent of bank holidays where scores of mods and rockers would cause chaos at the seaside, and with some well written and superbly produced songs designed to evoke that era's, this was the pinnacle of this aspect of Roy's songwriting and despite a re-issue on Edsel in the late 90's complete with all non-album singles and B-sides, it wasn't available until a remaster with bonus tracks released by Esoteric in 2020.

While being far less 'out there' than Wizzard Brew, is a wonderfully evocative record, featuring some of Roy's finest songwriting. The tracks are shorter, the band is reined in a lot tighter, but there is so much complexity and musical dexterity in these shorter tracks, representing different examples of Wood's musical vision. It is a testament to his skill as both the writer and producer of the album.

It never grabbed me at the time as much as *Wizzard Brew* would do a few years later, but time has been kinder to it than I realised, and when I heard the (the now out of print) two-CD set from *Sanctuary Look Thru' The Eyes of Roy Wood* which is a pretty comprehensive collection of the 1974-1987 period, the *Eddy* tracks on there caused me to dig out my old vinyl and revisit the record. With hindsight, I can understand exactly where Roy was coming from and what he was looking to achieve.

The Eddy-Era Singles
'Rock n Roll Winter (Looneys Tune)' (Wood) b/w 'Dream Of Unwin' (Grima)
Warner Brothers
Released 1974
Highest UK Chart position: 6
For line up see *Eddie And The Falcons*
Available on the Esoteric reissue of the album

Recorded and released in mono, this seasonal track – its release was delayed by several weeks until the end of March – was dedicated to Roy's then-girlfriend Lyndsey De Paul.

Carrying on the trend set by the previous four singles, this was the fifth release to hit the top ten in the UK and featured the line-up that released Introducing *Eddy and the Falcons,* and this is very much in that albums vein. Where some of the more interesting musical stylings of the previous singles are pared down slightly to a straight forward rock and roll homage, the plucking strings and Midlands wall of sound is very much on display.

Lyrically, this is a very upbeat and honest piece of songwriting, with Roy using his best crooning voice, and some fantastic sax runs from the band. The emphasis is very much on the songs rather than the musical intensity of *Wizzard Brew*. Very much a homage and influenced by the sound of classic 1950s/1960s big rock and roll ballads, this certainly indicated the direction in which *Eddy and the Falcons* would take Wizzard, and is more focused on a specific musical direction than the wayward but exciting musical stylings of *Wizzard Brew*. With a more polished production, some of the band's rough edges have been knocked off, but it certainly shows the knack Roy has for writing hit singles.

The B-side follows the pattern of letting band members write the flipside and is plaintive piano and synth-driven track. As it was written by Charlie Grima it is understandably percussion-heavy, and the synth sounds are incredibly modern for this era, sounding as it does more like a Moody Blues instrumental break, before a Spanish guitar solo arrives.

This is all incredibly un-Wizzard like, but a brief burst of vocals, an oboe solo and suitably spacey synth sound, it seems to foreshadow the sound palette that Wizzard would eventually create on the *Main Street* album.

'This Is The Story Of My Love (Baby)' (Wood) b/w 'Nixture' (Nick Pentelow)

Warner Brothers
Released 1974
Highest UK Chart Position: 34
For line up see *Eddie And The Falcons*
Available on the Esoteric reissue of the album

The lead single from the album was released in July 1974 and reached a disappointing 34 in the charts, breaking Wizzard's top ten record up until then. More detailed information on this song can be found in its entry on the album.

The B-side was written by Nick Pentelow and this is a very old-school, improvisational, instrumental jazz track. It's 1940s swing sax, and percussive sound, show the influence that the musical tastes of both Pentelow and Mike Burney would have on Roy Wood. It's duelling sax and smooth groove make it sound like a lost piece from 1970s a movie soundtrack.

'Are You Ready To Rock?' (Wood) b/w 'Marathon Man' (Mike Tyler/ Keith Smart)

Warner Brothers
Released: December 1974

Highest UK Chart Position 8
Line up as Introducing Eddy and the Falcons
Available on the Esoteric reissue of the album

This song, released in December 1974 after the release of the album, saw the band return to the UK top ten, although any hope of this being a permanent return were to be dashed, as this was sadly Wizzard's last appearance in the UK single charts with an original release, bringing the curtain down on an impressive seven-year run from The Move, ELO, Wizzard and Roy as a solo artist.

As throughout the *Eddy* era, this is a far more focused piece of rock and roll writing. Starting with a nod to Chuck Berry and Glen Miller, there is some 1940s swing brass, with twanging guitar and call and answer vocals and it has a real traditional swing and jive feel to it. There's some great sax work from the band and some rocking vocals from Roy, not to mention references to Eddy and the Falcons in the lyrics, so this closes out this era quite specifically. 1974 being the year of Eddy, and of course, in typically Roy fashion it bows out with a manic folky bagpipe solo, mixing the sound of swing and folk together successfully more than twenty years before Ashley Hutchings did with his folk-rock all-stars. It feels like this track was closure for this of music style that Wizzard had perfected, and with the bagpipes sneaking in, it has the whole 'end of term' feel to it, almost as if the decks were being cleared ready for the next direction of Wizzard.

As for the B-side, it is written by second drummer Keith Smart and non-band member Mike Tyler. This two-minute sitar and synth-driven instrumental sees the band flexing their musical chops and letting loose with some free form musical stylings, reminiscent of the instrumental sections on *Wizzard Brew*. These B-sides allowed the band space to stretch and create sounds that wouldn't necessarily end up on the album and are as essential to understanding the complexity and versatility of Wizzard as the albums and A-sides of the singles.

Introducing Eddy And The Falcons (album)

Personnel:
Roy Wood: vocal, electric guitars, sitar, cello, bassoon, baritone saxophone, string bass, Bb Bass Tuba, trombone, recorders, percussion, euphonium and military drums
Rick Price: bass guitar, vocals and percussion
Bill Hunt: piano.
Nick Pentelow: tenor saxophone, clarinet and flute, bass, backing vocals
Mike Burney: alto, tenor baritone and synthesised saxes, clarinets and flute
Keith Smart: drums
Charlie Grima: drums, congas, percussion
Bob Brady: keyboards and vocals
All tracks written and produced by Roy Wood

Warner Brothers
Released: August 1974
Highest UK Chart Position: 19
Available on Esoteric Records, 2020

'Intro'

The short opener to the album sets the scene for the band, starting with some dialogue about how great Eddy looks. A faux live intro follows, complete with screaming and some great introductory guitar this segues nicely into...

'Eddy's Rock'

Taking as it's starting point the fictitious band Eddy and the Falcons, this allows the band to step to one side from being Wizzard and take on a slightly different musical persona.

Similar to what the Beatles were attempting with *Sgt Pepper*, this deliberately evokes the memories of a specific era of Rock 'n' Roll, and this instrumental start to the album has some big meaty riffs, picking up, once again, almost where 'California Man' left off. This and the guitar work are reminiscent of the burst of creativity that typified that last era of The Move.

The duel solos of saxes and guitars help build this driving rocking song, complete with some Duane Eddy licks, some funky guitar work and acoustic fingerpicking. This takes the instrumental dexterity from the debut album but focuses it right down so that the band are a lot tighter and punchier than on their debut.

'Brand New '88'

American cars – and car-based rock and roll – are something that Roy would return to later in his career. But here, each track on this album is finely crafted and shaped to fit a specific musical moment in time. The sound of this album is the whole 1950s / 1960s rock 'n' roll awakening, a zeitgeist the movie *Grease* was to tap into a few years later. Here, with some rocking piano, guitar riffs, honking sax, this is – literally – a driving rock song. There are images of teenage freedom and again comes from the same mould as 'California Man'. A rollicking Bob Brady piano solo apes the intensity that 'the killer' (Jerry Lee Lewis) brought to his performances, while Roy's rock vocals are superb here. Additionally, the dual saxes of Mike Burney and Nick Pentelow are all over this track, with some fantastic soloing and the tautness of their sound really makes this album swing.

'You Got Me Runnin''

Switching mood and styles, complete with 'sha la la la's', this is pure teen idol pop at it's finest, sitting at the point where doo-wop meets pop, emulating many of the teen crooners and songwriters. Doffing its hat to Goffin and King and Neil Sedaka, Roy's smooth croon over the descending bass, handclap percussion, and the double drum percussive power that underpins this whole track makes this an impressive homage to that specific era. Lyrics like 'hippety hop all over the world' and the percussive breakdown, where we just hear the vocals and percussion, are very impressive. There's also a nod to Buddy Holly vocally meaning that this track bounces along with energy and is a lot of fun.

'I Dun Lotsa Cryin' Over You'

This album really is a lesson in classic rock and roll, as well as a whistle-stop tour across the United States Of America. Here we enjoy a stopover at Memphis and Sun Studios. This song is as perfect a homage to early Elvis as I've heard. The instrumentation is sparse, with some swinging bass and Roy pulls off a superb Elvis impression. A wonderfully simple solo, and that doo-wop shuffle underpinning the song this is a very close cousin to the rockabilly swing of 'Don't Mess Me Up' from *Message From the Country*. Of any album in Roy's musical history, this album, with its taut production, focused songwriting and performances, and the way it just rocks throughout, suggests that it is the ultimate statement of where The Move were heading in 1972. Rounding off the track is a wonderfully jaunty little piano break from Bob Brady, whose piano sound is a massive part of what makes this album so impressive.

'This Is The Story Of My Love (Baby)'

Here's a rarity. This is the only Wizzard single to also feature on an album (excluding compilations, of course) and was also the first single by the band not to reach the top ten, breaking their run of big hits. Listening back now, it's very difficult to understand why it didn't do better. Full of lush orchestration and instrumentation, this is Roy at his most melodic – a big old rock and roll ballad in the mould of 'Angel Fingers'. It has a full-on wall of sound production, 'la la la' backing vocals, teen pop lyrics and, pulling out all the stops, the band are as tight as they ever were.

Again, with the instrumentation, vocal harmonies, and even a bassoon solo, this is the perfect combination of Roy's work on *Looking On* and the more complex *Wizzard Brew* tracks. It matches the style of the band's debut singles, as well as forming part of the overreaching Eddy and the Falcons narrative, so this sounds the perfect choice for a single from the album, and it feels like the big hit that got away. This is Roy Wood at his finest, and with the closing sax solos is as near perfect a three-minute symphony as you'll find anywhere.

'Everyday I Wonder'

Here Roy channels his inner Del Shannon, complete with a haunting symphony and jangling guitar, percussive backing track, and haunting, plaintive vocals. This inevitably means that this song might be compared to the iconic Shannon trick 'Runaway', which was the intention no doubt. In fact, it's the mood of the darker tones of that song that this evokes, rather than being a mere copy or pastiche. Dramatic descending piano chords, emotive and heavy guitar riffs and the unstoppable motion of the song also remind us in parts of 'It Wasn't My Idea To Dance', again from *Message from the Country*. There's a great difference between 'simplicity' and 'uncomplicated'. The dense musical layering, the emotive lyrics and the controlled tension throughout this song is a masterclass in how to tell a complete story within a five-minute window. The woodwind solo, piano break and choral sections, and, indeed, Roy's impassioned vocals, also suggest elements of 'The Words of Aaron', particularly as the song builds to its impressive musical climax. Had this song been a single, it would no doubt have been a hit and is an example of what Roy could achieve as a producer and songwriter. It is the highlight of the album.

'Crazy Jeans'
Changing the mood and the dynamic again, this song opens with a Fats Domino-style piano and some Chuck Berry guitar. It is a shuffling rocker, complete with a Bob Brady vocal, some really neat finger-picked soloing and is the perfect way to switch the mood. This is the sort of song that pop stars like Shakin' Stevens would attempt to pastiche in the early 1980s, but without the style and aplomb that Wizzard pull off here. That guitar tone is perfect, while the frenetic drumming and bass work of Rick Price really brings in that energy and rawness of those early rock and roll records, and again strips the sound right back, before the piano breaks return to fade.

'Come Back Karen'
This is another nod to the work of Neil Sedaka. The track is a slower bossa nova, complete with higher-register vocals of Wood, based around plinking strings and plaintive broken-hearted vocals. Descending mournful saxes, bass shuffle and the show-band-style drumming sound, bring the idea of the slow dance at the school prom to mind here. It's not hard to imagine the band playing this, dressed in their drapes and with their hair slicked back, while teenagers try to waltz slowly on the dance floor. The sax solo in the middle of this song is sublime, while the imagery and mood it evokes work wonderfully in the context of this album, as the moods ebb and flow, and the music ends with the perfect 1950s 'cha cha cha'.

'We're Gonna Rock 'n Roll Tonight'
This is the big, closing rocker. Wood, Price and Brady trade vocals and a mammoth riff drives this track. There are references to New Orleans, and with some powerful dual percussion, this is the perfect way to round the record off, as if it was a live show, leaving the big rocker to the end. There is some amazingly some powerful vocal work from the band, with massive sax sounds, and a real funky backbeat.

With a heavy bass riff from Rick Price, and the trio singing with different vocal styles, combining into a raucous chorus, this is a different sound to the lush harmonies from earlier and pushes the bands sound right at the end of the rock spectrum – a far cry from the smooth dance style of the previous song. Which is the point, as the musicians riff, trade licks and solos over the extended fade. There is more of that wonderfully authentic piano work and this track is the only one on the album that has that out of control feeling that you get running through *Wizzard Brew*, ending up on wonderfully spaced out synthesiser. It is a masterclass in controlled chaos.

The Interim Singles
'Rattlesnake Roll' b/w 'Can't Help My Feelings'
Written and produced by Roy Wood
Released by Jet records October 1975
Currently unavailable

Featuring some of Bob Brady's fantastic pub room piano boogie-woogie, in the sort of style that Jools Holland would be plying us with on British TV some 30 years later, this single was released in 1975 and credited to Wizzard. It is a continuation of the themes found throughout Eddy and the Falcons, and has a real 1950s swing and jive sound, with Bob Brady on vocals with Roy. This is another rocker that strips the sound right back, driven by the piano and swinging, big band bass, along with a stabbing brass arrangement. It is almost the last gasp of that particular style of songwriting that Roy had been working with. While it is an entertaining little rocker, it does seem to be a little bit of a backwards step in the context of the way Roy's career and musical vision was developing, apart from the slide guitar finale which hints at sounds to come on *Main Street*.

The B-side is a complete opposite to it's A-side, being a contemporary piece of smooth funk, with vocals again by Bob Brady, bringing the song far closer to the Wizzo/Main Street sound than it's single. A contemporary groove built up by the band allow Brady to flex his vocal cords, and the group build up a great head of steam with a powerful riff by Wood, some really catchy vocals. It has a polished, driving beat and its female backing vocals make this follow the ideal of 'Feel Too Good', condensed, updated and with a radio-friendly FM sheen, that hints at the sophistication and sound that would characterise *Main Street*. There is a nice little bagpipe/oboe breakdown mixed with a nifty guitar riff and slide guitar work that builds on the more experimental side of Wizzard, and this finishes this hidden gem off nicely, with some fantastic musical interplay between the band. While there are no credits as to who does what, it wouldn't be unreasonable to assume that the *Main Street* band are on here somewhere.

'Indiana Rainbow' b/w 'The Thing Is (This Is The Thing)'
Written and produced by Roy Wood
Released by Jet Records 1976
Chart position: didn't chart

Availability: currently unavailable
Line up as *Main Street* album

Credited to Roy and Wizzard and tagged as being from the forthcoming album 'Wizzo', 'Indian Rainbow' is indicative of the style that Roy had been heading towards. *Main Street*, the album it finally became part of, recorded in 1976 but not released until 1999, was for many years a lost classic, as discussed shortly.

Unavailable for so many years like its A-side, this expansive instrumental B-side (why break the habit of a lifetime) see's the band stretching and flexing their jazz muscles in full. What had previously been hinted at on other B-sides is given free rein here, as the bass and saxes intermingle. Indeed, using bass as a lead instrument is something bands like Yes had been doing for years, but this is a new approach for Roy. The mix of guitar, synth, bass and drums all sound very much more progressive in terms of genre rather than attitude and stretch out how adventurous the band had been on B-sides before to new lengths. There is some serious groove going down on here and some really nifty fingerpicking as well, as the piece turns and flows through various genres, before coming into land with the original sax riff repeated.

Sounding more like a Yes vs ELP vs Mahavishnu Orchestra face-off than a Wizzard track, this really pointed the listener in the direction of travel for the forthcoming album *Wizzo*, which, as we all know, didn't make it out in 1976 as planned.

Roy Wood and Wizzard: Main Street (album)
All songs written, arranged and produced by Roy Wood.
Recording engineer: Dick Plant
Recorded in 1976 at the Music Centre, Wembley, England
Roy Wood: lead vocal, guitars, backing vocals, saxophones, oboe, string bass, French horn, electric sitar, bass clarinet, electronic keyboards, bass guitar, drums.
Rick Price: bass, pedal steel guitar
Charlie Grima: drums, congas, percussion, vocals on 'Don't You Feel Better'
Bob Brady: piano
Nick Pentelow: saxes, flutes
Mike Burney: saxes, flutes
Richard Plant: vocals on 'Take My Hand'
Remastered by Roy Wood & Roger Lomas at Ro-Lo Studios 2000.
Currently available on Esoteric 2020.
Highest UK Chart position: Didn't Chart

Eddy was originally planned as a double album, with the rock and roll album as record one, and the new jazz-tinged sound of the songs that eventually became *Main Street* as disc two. Warner Bros preferred the rock and roll sound, so persuaded the band to record Eddy alone.

By the time that Roy and the remnants of Wizzard came to record the album that was to become *Main Street*, they were signed to Jet records. The lead single was 'Indiana Rainbow', which was totally different from anything that Roy had released before was released in 1976 under Roy Wood and Wizzard and trailed as coming from the new album *Wizzo*. This never materialised and the Jet executives decided not to release the 'Wizzo' recordings. The next thing anyone would hear from Roy would be in 1977 with the *Super Active Wizzo* album, the culmination of his jazz-rock 'odyssey'. If listening to *Super Active Wizzo* sounded like it was something new and different to Roy Wood fans, then listening to this lost album, finally released in 2000 as *Main Street,* is the missing piece.

It's the connection between the Wizzard albums and *Super Active Wizzo*, and it's astonishing that a complete album of material by someone as important as Roy Wood could have lain unreleased on for just over 23 years until Edsel remastered and released it. We will discuss it in order of recording rather than release because this is part of the evolution of Roy's sound, and it's easier to understand *Wizzo* after hearing *Main Street*. One or two tracks would sneak out as B-sides, but the album finally made its debut as Roy intended, at the turn of the century.

Listening back now, *Main Street* has some flaws. It is also as different from its predecessor as it is possible to be without it being the work of a different band entirely. You must admire Roy for trying to evolve and grow his songwriting style into textures that fit more with what he was listening to at the time and what he wanted to play rather than being driven by commercial demands. It's a shame that the Record label didn't have the courage of their convictions and let this album be released as *Wizzo* as it was intended.

'Main Street'

This is a smooth, sax driven track, mixing crooning vocals with a piano-driven, almost Beach Boys-like vocal delivery. Gone are the manic drums and the crazier instrumentation of the Wizzard days. Instead, this is a far more sophisticated sound. The track brings in some big band sounds, some piano work from Bob Brady (who had been stellar in the latter days of Wizzard), and has a much more AOR sheen on the production. This was a far more laid back take on Roy's sound, but the trademark vocal harmonies are still there, always one of Roy's strengths. There are other familiar tropes as well, including the American infatuation in terms of the lyrics and that mix of slick pop and jazz instrumentation. In the sleeve notes that Roy wrote for the Edsel edition (1999) he commentated that:

> This was probably a last attempt to retain some sort of sanity, trying to grow up and not carry on indefinitely being another pop group.

'Saxmaniax'

This takes the instrumental ideas that Roy used as B-sides and expands them. In fact, 'Saxmaniax' is the only other *Main Street* song after 'Indiana

Rainbow' to have been commercially issued contemporaneously, as a B-side ironically enough. It takes a pounding driving beat, then, as the title suggests, crams it full of some wonderful, duelling sax work from Roy and long term collaborators Nick Pentelow and Mike Burney. It builds into an extremely slick groove again, but stripping back some of the more 'out there' instrumentation, it is still identifiably Wizzard.

'The Fire In His Guitar'
The Longest track on the album clocking in at seven-plus minutes, this is another song to play to anyone who might be surprised by the progressive side of Roy's career. It mixes some powerful riffing more akin to Tony Iommi or Eric Clapton than what you'd normally associate with Roy and has some incredible solo's throughout. The length of the song allows it to build and sneaking in some 'Strangers In The Night' into one of the riffs, shows that Roy still had a little bit of twinkle in the eye, while pushing this harder and heavier soundscape.

There's some nice instrumentation work at about three minutes in, mixing the drum, bass and guitar and there are changes in tempo and style as the sax returns, bringing that big band sound again. However, they effortlessly switch back into the powerhouse riffing, without dropping a beat, indicating that this is the sound that the band have been wanting to play with for ages. The track takes the disparate elements of the previous B-sides, adds some real Midlands steel into the sound and production and the whole cocktail comes across as the mix between Mahavishnu Orchestra, Black Sabbath and Slade. Indeed, the extended solos and workouts here are never self-indulgent or contrived. Instead, they build up to a head of steam with a real groove and the foundation of the drums and bass provided by Rick Price and Charlie Grima really anchor the piece, allowing the track to ebb and flow as the tempo builds.

This is the Wizzard brew finely distilled and matured for three years.

'French Perfume'
A more traditional Roy Wood ballad, with some excellent piano work by Bob Brady, this switches between a laid back 40s shuffle (not dissimilar to some of the elements of *Mustard*) while the saxes flit around, between some deft fingerpicking on the acoustic guitar from Roy. Instead of showing off his multi-instrumental abilities, on some of these tracks, Roy focuses on instruments and sounds, and the smooth fingerpicking on the acoustic gives a totally different timbre to the solo, adding to the vaudeville-meets-big-band-meets-Wizzard vibe that is conjured up here. When you look at the variety of instruments he plays around with and his versatility as a songwriter and performer, it's easy to forget that Roy honed his craft on the guitar and this album features some brilliant examples of his guitar playing, both acoustic and electric.

'Take My Hand'

There are far fewer out and out rockers on this album than on previous records, showing perhaps the maturity of Roy's songwriting, and of course the fact that the band were moving into a more sophisticated direction. This is a classic big ballad, following in the vein of tracks like 'Whisper in the Night' and 'Dear Elaine' and this piano-driven softer piece, always feels like it's threatening to build into something else. The fact it is kept restrained and more low key, is testament to the arrangements and performances.

Haunting, eerie synths float and shimmer across the track and give it an otherworldly feel, while the sax that emotes across the breaks suggests the Hazel O'Conner song 'Stay Now' from almost a decade later. This, with its refined production and radio-friendly elements, could have been a successful single had it been released in 1976 and is one of the bona fide lost classics on this album.

'Don't You Feel Better'

Upping the tempo again, this has a lot more of the funk and groove, with Rick Price and Charlie Grima working in tandem peerlessly. Vocals on this cut are provided by Richard Plant who adds a real soulful vibe. The groove and the way that the beat builds on this one, particularly the saxes and pounding drum beat recalls 'Feels Too Good'. This is another example of Roy writing a slightly different love song, and while this rocks, it's far more subtle than an all-out, in your face sonic attack. Here, the instrumentation is used tactically, and the beat has a real element of drive and funk, making this is more reminiscent of the Average White Band and the wonderful call and response chorus, in tandem with the building sax and bass, is a musical tour de force.

'Indiana Rainbow'

This was the lead single, and again it sounds nothing like any single Roy had released before. This is as smooth as 'Main Street'. Roy's unique vocals are to the fore, and instead of some massive, catchy hook, this is far more sophisticated in its melody and production style.

Taking away a lot of the 'in your face' element that Wizzard had been known for, this song has a catchy little intro played on flutes by Pentelow and Burney (reminiscent of 'Curly') while the song is structured ever so slightly differently, without a standard 'big' chorus. It mixes vocal harmonies, sneaks in elements of the 'Sugarplum Fairy' and has some very restrained guitar solos, while the drumbeat is metronomic, powering the track on.

As sophisticated and mature as this is, it was showcasing a side of Roy's songwriting that had only previously been hinted at on B-sides. It had hardly set the world on fire at the time and was an indication that while Roy was trying to move on musically, the rest of the industry wanted to keep him in the same box. This was a great shame, as Roy said from the *Main Street* booklet in 2000:

I would like to believe that, if this album had been released when it was first created, then my writing style would have taken a different curve and we would have been performing the type of material that bands such as Jamiroquai are being successful with right now.

'I Should Have Known'

With a funky guitar riff that sounds like a distant cousin of 'Ticket to Ride' seen through the eyes of John McLaughlin and a sax wall of sound driving this song, this is one of the rockier songs on the album. There is a duelling solo element where the saxes and Roy's guitar intertwine over a slick grove. The bass and drums again work dextrously and are part of what makes this album work, with Price and Grima the beating hearts on this record. This allows the rest of the band the freedom to mix up the sound, while Roy cracks out the sitar which adds another of his trademark sounds to the mix. Ending on this funky take on a rock song, finishes off a huge missing chapter in the Roy Wood story.

Bonus Track
'Human Cannonball'

Previously only available on the Sanctuary compilation *Lookin' thru the Eyes of Roy Wood,* and recorded during the Main Street sessions, the sleeve notes to the Esoteric remaster state that Roy didn't want it included on the original *Main Street* release. It's hard to understand why as it's an absolute classic Woody rocker, with a heavy riff, some great soloing from Roy and a pounding, intense performance from the band that sounds like they are on the brink of veering out of control, not to mention Roy's full on rock vocals. It's great to have it back where it belongs.

Roy Wood's Wizzo Band: Super Active Wizzo (album)

Personnel:
Roy Wood: vocals, guitars, tenor, baritone, soprano and alto saxes electric sitar, clavinet, bass and string bass, Moog, vocal backing.
Dave Donovan: drums
Billy Paul: Alto and Baritone Saxes
Graham Gallery: Bass
Rick Price: Pedal steel guitar and electric guitar
Bob Wilson: trombone
Paul Robbins: backing vocals (now playing keyboards with the Wizzo Band)
All songs by Roy Wood except where indicated and published by Jet Music/Carlin
Album arranged and produced by Roy Wood
Recorded at De Lane Lea Studios Wembley
Engineered by Dick Plant and Mike Pela with Barry (Baz) Kidd assistant Engineer
Released by Warner Brothers, September 1977
Highest UK Chart position: didn't chart.
Currently only available as digital download. No physical release.

This album is the culmination of his jazz/rock experimentation that started as Wizzard sax men Nick Pentelow and Mike Burney introduced Roy to jazz during the band's longer tours. It had influenced his songwriting on the album that became *Main Street*, as well as throughout the different B-sides written by the various members of Wizzard that allowed the band to stretch out and start to bring new influences to bear on their sound.

This finally saw him breaking out of the 'pop star' box he'd ended up stuck in during the early 1970s and was a more honest reflection of how rounded a performer and writer he had become.

While the album is a departure from what many considered his trademark sound, let's not forget how eclectic and exciting a performer and writer Roy was – and remains – from the proto-metal on *Shazam,* the soul and progressive rock that runs through *Looking On* and the insane conclusion of psychedelia that became The Electric Light Orchestra. Roy has always been a writer who hasn't just pushed the envelope but has totally relocated the stationery store.

The Wizzo band, which toured heavily prior to the release of this album, recorded a *Sight and Sound* concert for the BBC, which is currently unavailable. It featured stalwart Rick Price, switching back to guitar, who became Roy's longest-serving musical compadre and a new band with a more fluid, jazzy feel to it. The album also saw a couple of co-writes, with Renaissance vocalist Annie Haslam and drummer Dave Donovan.

The last album released by Roy in the UK in the 1970s, *Super Active Wizzo,* with it's washing powder inspired logo, and Roy and a guitar as a mad axeman, didn't impact upon the charts and was the last album he released as part of a band. Part of the problem for this record is there's too much extended musical exploration that doesn't go anywhere near as far as the breakouts on *Wizzard Brew* or *Mustard* and with its big band feel, it's trying to be too grown up. Indeed, the thing that is missing on this album is the sense of fun and tongue in cheek playfulness that characterises many of his other records.

While there are some good tracks on here, they tend to go on for too long without a satisfying conclusion and there's not enough of a mix in contrasts and tempos. While it's not hard to appreciate what Roy was trying to achieve with this album, unfortunately, it doesn't quite hit its mark and I prefer the diversity of the *Main Street* album. *Super Active Wizzo* as a record that is more to be admired rather than loved, and it is such a shame as there is so much potential, but it doesn't quite work. But even a slightly misfiring album by Roy Wood is a damn sight better than many full-blown albums by other artists, as even though it doesn't always quite work, there are more musical ideas on here than other artists have in their entire careers.

'Life is Wonderful' (Wood)
If *Main Street* had been released as *Wizzo*, as originally intended, then this opener wouldn't have come as much as a surprise. It features a full-on brass arrangement and a nagging, insistent groove, married with a fluid guitar riff

more reminiscent of improvisational bands than Wizzard. Mixed with some traditional-style vocals from Roy, this is one of the freer form openers on any of his albums. It's also an expansive eight minutes long, taking plenty of time for the groove to play out and the mix of stabbing brass, electric guitar solos and harmony vocals make this song's construction more like fusion band Colosseum than like any of Roy's contemporaries Slade or The Electric Light Orchestra. In fact, like former bandmate Jeff Lynne's movement away from symphonies to rock songs with strings, this track sees Roy veer in totally the opposite direction, putting brass and jazz-influenced sounds into longer songs and soundscapes. Indeed, this is as progressive as the debut ELO album, and see's Roy taking his brass-inspired vision to its logical musical conclusion.

'Waitin' At This Door' (Wood)

This track opens with a mammoth riff that circles and builds, while the drumming of Dave Donovan powers the song. Mixing choral vocals with Rick Price's slide guitar, this song sounds like it could have been recorded by Yes at several points in their career. There are also stabbing strings, and a nod to disco in the second verse, but the slide guitar dominates proceedings, as the mood switches. The song is very up-tempo and sees various musical techniques from earlier songs return, such as the strings and brass intertwining, technically complex guitar parts and Roy's rock vocals to the fore.

Some of the vocal effects also recall of the jazzier elements to Zappa's work in the 1970s, and we know that Roy was a massive Zappa fan. With all its complexities and switches between styles, this is a song that takes a while to get into, especially with a random-sounding country and western break, before the song launches back into the chorus.

Indeed, the same can be said of the entire album, as there are no big riffs or songs that just grab the listener immediately. Instead, this is a slow burn; an album packed full of complexities and subtle nuances that are teased out, track by track. Even *Wizzard Brew* still had many catchy moments, so to fans who were more familiar with the catchy riff and hook-laden work of Wizzard, this must have been received as a complete about-turn.

'Another Wrong Night' (Wood)

This is another long track at over eleven minutes and has a guitar part and introduction reminiscent of *Main Street*. Indeed, Its style of writing and singing would follow through to *On the Road Again*. Again, Wood was stretching his songwriting out, although there was plenty of precedent for this – just turn to *Looking On* or *Shazam* to see that Roy was no stranger to extended musical workouts.

However, instead of these being full-on psychedelic wig-outs, as with those albums, these tracks are more structured and arranged for the full band, rather than Roy and Jeff seemingly making it up as they went along. This track is also very much 'of its time', sounding very much like this were a BBC house band in the 1970s, with its structured brass, jangling guitar and stabbing brass. The guitar, drum and bass interplay is great around the five-minute mark. However, the track itself does tend to meander along in a pedestrian fashion and for eleven minutes of music, there isn't enough deviation and excitement. Compare this to the ten minutes of 'Wear A Fast Gun' or the nine minutes plus of 'Feel Too Good', and you'll understand, and while it's a pleasant enough song, it never gets out of third gear.

'Sneakin'' (Wood)

This song is a bit livelier, with some of that wonderful 1940s brass sound that Roy snuck into so many of his songs. The drumming, again, is fairly powerful, and the vocals are incredibly soulful. However, the problem with this song, like so many on this album, is that it never quite kicks into overdrive. Moments that might be bigger, louder and more epic instead fade away into the slicker, smoother style that was present across *Main Street*. It's almost like it's been produced too democratically, 'this is the brass section' 'this is the bass breakdown' 'here's the keyboard solo' and while the musicianship is superb, even though Roy's vocals are on point as ever. Unfortunately, like a lot of tracks, this one could have been improved by editing down and taking out a lot of the meandering. It feels like it wants to go somewhere, but never quite seems to get there, which is a shame,

'Giant Footsteps (Jubilee)' (Roy Wood, Annie Haslam, Dave Donovan)

B-side from the only single released from this album, this piece follows Roy and Wizzard's tradition for releasing instrumentals as B-Sides. This co-write with drummer Dave Donovan and (strangely) singer Annie Haslam, is a very funk-driven piece, where the sitar and synth battle it out over a drum and bass riff which is very 1977. With its stabs of brass and its sax breaks, it comes across as part old Wizzard B-side, and part American cop-show theme.
Indeed, the bass and brass sound like they dropped out off a James Bond soundtrack while the slow groove that the band creates ticks along nicely as the various instrumentalists pull out a solo here or there. There's even a drum solo, something of a 70s cliché. Overall, this is a very pleasant piece of music, but nothing that is memorable.

'Earthrise' (Roy Wood, Dick Plant)

Again, this is another eleven minute plus epic. We know Roy uses the final track as the big epic, but on an album full of epics, how do you finish the record? It opens with some great guitar work, and some new age lyrics, mixing more of his sitar work and a metronomic drum beat reminiscent in parts to 'Feel Too Good'. It has a great yearning vocal from Roy and some of the rockier riffs on the album, however, once again, it's a tad too repetitive and meandering, making a potentially-great song less than inspiring.

Singles:
'The Stroll' (Wood) **b/w 'Giant Footsteps '(Jubilee)'** (Wood, Haslam, Donovan)
Released by Warner Brothers in 1977
Chart position: didn't chart.
Availability: 'The Stroll' is currently unavailable, but can be heard on YouTube.
'Giant Footsteps (Jubilee)' – available on *Super Active Wizzo* download only.

The only single credited to Roy Wood's Wizzo band is a far funkier piece of music than the tracks on the Wizzo album, with some great Motown style horns, and a riff reminiscent of Stevie Wonder. There's some really powerful percussion from Dave Donovan, and some fine slide guitar throughout from Rick Price, who, through his stints in The Move and Wizzard and The Wizzo band remains Roy's longest-serving musical collaborator on record and some of Roys harder-edged rock vocals. This is a fine blend of contemporary soul and funk, and mixes the rock sensibilities of Roys songwriting, with a fine old school 1950s piano-led section. Lyrically, the song has a lot in common with 'Brontosaurus' – it's again about a new dance style – with some fine drum breaks throughout. However, it was as about as out of sync as is possible for 1977, the year where Roy's old band ELO finally went stratospheric and when disco, not punk, ruled the airwaves. Had it been released two years earlier it might have made more of an impact, however by 1977 any public interest in Roy had waned, which is a pity as this is a very sophisticated slice of songwriting.

'Dancin' At The Rainbows End' b/w 'Waiting At This Door'
Written and produced by Roy Wood
Released by Warner Bros
Highest UK Chart position: didn't chart
Availability: 'Dancin' At The Rainbows End' available on *On the Road Again* (see that section for details)
'Waitin' At The Door' available on *Super Active Wizzo* digital download.

I have discussed both these songs separately under their individual albums and 'Dancin' at the Rainbows End' finally appearing as part of *On the Road Again*, bridging the gap between the Wizzo band and the resumption of Roy's solo career.

6. Roy Wood – The Solo Albums

Astonishingly, across his career, Roy has only released four solo albums, the last one being 1986's *Starting Up*. These four albums show different sides of Roy. The songs are more personal and have different arrangements than those he might put together for the bands he was in at the time. However, with these recordings – solo and band – all happening at the same time, and some albums being released long after they were recorded, it's difficult to get the full picture of his solo work.

I aim to untangle some of the chronology, look at the individual albums, and wonder why, not for the first time, that someone as supremely talented (and who continues to perform sell-out tours to this day!) still isn't producing new material, and has large parts of his musical career unavailable on physical format. Roy was so prolific – even at the end of the 1970s and early 1980s when he was outside of his commercial peak – that he continued to release stand-alone singles, which are also covered here.

The Roy Wood Original Album Series, is a misnomer, as it features *Message From The Country* (by The Move – in its original album form without any of the bonus tracks on the long-deleted 2005 remaster), ELO's first album (with no bonus tracks), *Boulders* (again the basic version) and finally *On the Road Again*, which has never even had a remastered release and is currently unavailable in physical form outside this box. A Roy Wood fan might begrudge paying for a cardboard box to get albums they already own to get one or two that they don't. However, *Mustard* has had a recent re-release with bonus tracks on the Esoteric label, while *Boulders* is available on 180-gram vinyl and *Starting Up* is only available to stream or download after a brief rerelease on CD via the Sanctuary label.

As the labels Roy had signed and released music through, via mergers, acquisitions and other music business shenanigans now come under the Warner Music label, then its time that someone worked on a comprehensive and complete remastering process, putting everything Roy worked on from *Message to the Country* onwards back out there, to reflect his legacy. We should all give a huge thanks to the Esoteric label for making a good start over the last few years since some of the Edsel remasters in the late 1990s. Aside from the five-CD box, *On The Road Again* is only available to download or stream.

Of course, The Move is an important part of Roy's musical legacy, but there is so much more to him as a writer and a performer than The Move and the hit singles with Wizzard. While the solo albums aren't fully available, it's like the full story isn't being heard.

Boulders (album)

All titles composed by Roy Wood.
Personnel:
All instruments by Roy Wood except harmonium on 'Songs of Praise' by John

Kurlander
Recorded at EMI Studios and Phonogram Studios London
Produced by Roy Wood,
Released on Harvest in the UK and United Artists in the US in August 1973
Chart position UK: 15 US: 176 (*Billboard* 200)
Availability: Currently only available in *Roy Wood The Original Album Series*
Parlophone/Warner Brothers 2014 and on 180 gm vinyl

Astonishingly, Roy's debut album *Boulders* (which first saw a CD release
back in 1994 on boutique reissue label BGO, owned by Andy Grey of Andy's
records) was recorded in 1969, in between *Shazam*, and *Looking On*, and
is a solo album in all respects. Every instrument was played by Roy, and all
songs were written and produced by him as well. Despite the recordings being
ready to go, *Boulders* didn't get an official album release until 1973 on the
Harvest label and a full remaster back in 2006 also on Harvest which is now
no longer available. This meant that in 1972, you had the confusing situation
of the final batch of Move singles hitting the charts, ELO reaching the top ten
with '10538 Overture', Roy launching Wizzard with the hit single 'Ball Park
Incident', and then his debut solo single 'When Gran'ma Plays the Banjo', all
within three months.

Is there any wonder that it seemed in 1972 and 1973 Roy Wood was
ubiquitous?

The album demonstrated that all the pressures from being in bands like The
Move and the Electric Light Orchestra were not present in his solo work and
shows just how diverse and eclectic his tastes were, which is reflected in the
styles and sounds on display here.

I bought this back in March 1998, and until coming to write this book it had
been some years since I played it, the follow up solo album *Mustard* getting far
more time on the turntable. At the time, I was used to the more intricate and
intense sound of Wood's work with ELO and Wizzard. So, at a brief 39 minutes
long, the more simplistic arrangements at first seemed a bit disappointing
and tracks like 'When Gran'ma plays the Banjo', and 'Nancy Sing Me a Song'
seemed slight. It was easy to file the album under the 'interesting but not great'
category. But later, the homespun charms of this album hooked me completely.

This is Roy Wood in distilled to his essence. It is a solo album more in
common with low key works like *McCartney* than anything Roy recorded
with The Move, and even though he finds a home for the unfinished Move
track 'She's Too Good for Me (Second Class)', he still puts his own take on it.
Compare and contrast it with the version that's a bonus track on the current
Shazam reissue. With Roy in control, it's probably the closest to the perfect Roy
Wood musical vision than any we'd had so far at this point in his career.

This collection of tracks were the ones he obviously felt wouldn't fit into
either The Move or ELO and so kept them back, worked on them and it
gave him more freedom to play outside of the musical confines that the two

different bands had put him in. So, this is where Roy does some of his best work, out of the band confines and in the studio environment where he had the time to do just what he felt. As a result, this album was never going to be as highly rated as works like *Message from the Country* or *Wizzard Brew*, but in the context of Roy's career, but not every album ever made needs to be a grand statement, if it does what it needs to do.

The artwork for this album was a lot more sparse than previous albums, with the picture being Roy's hand-painted self-portrait (also used on The Move's *Message from the Country* cover) this time with his hair painted red and blue, to symbolise fire and water, shaking hands at the parting.

Boulders was reissued in 2007 with a rough guide version of 'Dear Elaine' but is sadly no longer available in that format. As a debut solo album, it was not made to herald the start of a solo career. Instead, it was more of a case of getting these songs recorded and released, as there were no other vehicles or projects that these songs would quite fit into. As such, it is an eclectic and eccentric collection, much like its creator, in which genres vary and styles mix and match. It's not so much a concept, and more a snapshot, the difference between old school photos and holiday snaps. Nonetheless, it works very well as a debut album and it's just unfortunate that with all the other projects that Roy was involved with at the time it got a little lost and it was hard to see where it fitted at the time. Now, its place in Roy's history is much better defined.

'Songs of Praise'
This charming little opener, complete with multi-tracked choral harmony vocals from Roy, was also recorded by The New Seekers and got through to the last six songs for their British entry to the 1972 *Eurovision Song Contest*. It's a funky, upbeat track with a straightforward riff, and Roy singing about songs of praise and belief. This showed a spiritual side to Roy, hitherto unseen, and has some tremendous folky piano, and an incredibly catchy chorus. It seems, on the surface, to be a light-hearted throwaway ditty, but in its own way has some quite deep lyrics, and sense of personal spirituality that makes it mark without being overtly preachy like some other 70s musicians (yes, John Lennon, I'm looking at you). Using studio trickery, that has Roy overdubbed and multi-tracked as a choir. He would return to using a full choir with even greater effect, later in his career.

'Wake Up'
This is a low key, acoustic love song, with sparse instrumentation, accompanied by a flute that soars beautifully. With the cello in the background and low in the mix, this track could easily have ended up on *Message from the Country*, matching that albums emphasis on pure songwriting and with the pastoral vibe it has. This follows one of the motifs of the early 1970s, which was about getting back to nature and the countryside and this is a far more pastoral and stripped back ballad than we'd seen from Roy before.

'Rock Down Low'

Influenced by rock n' roll, skiffle and the mods v rockers scene – something Roy would return to regularly – 'Rock Down Low' is a prime slice of Wood rock. Reminiscent of some of the rockier tracks on *Looking On*, it has some great woodwind solos, and plenty of booming sax, while Roy uses his great rock vocals to fine effect. A rather more playful track, this song uses a few tricks here that Roy would revisit in both Wizzard and the years of The Move. This isn't pastiching, though, showing his love of 1960s rock shows, but it's a fantastic homage in which he interprets the original style of rock 'n' roll through his own eclectic music vision.

'Nancy Sing Me A Song'

The jaunty beat of this song contrasts with its folky tone, so it's easy to imagine it coming to Roy around the same time as 'Curly', it has that same kind of light feel to it, with an arrangement based around acoustic guitar and light touches of cello. Roy sings about his emotions, with the song based around one of those female characters who often cropped up in The Move mythology, like the beautiful daughter, Suzie or the female protagonist in 'Here We Go Round The Lemon Tree'.

'Dear Elaine'

Released as a single b/w 'Songs Of Praise' in 1973
Highest UK chart position: 13

Elaine follows Nancy but the song is closer to 'Whisper In The Night' from The Electric Light Orchestra album, in that it has a more traditional ballad form. Roy declares his love for Elaine, who has spurned him. Underneath the song, the strings swell and soar, as Roy's versatile voice rises and falls in line with the instrumentation. There is a huge amount going on in the production and arrangement of this song and it's no surprise that it was chosen as the second single. Indeed, it is representative of the album and it's easy to forget that Roy is playing every instrument. From the baroque arrangements of the strings to the guitar work and the backing vocals, everything builds up from a slow start to a full crescendo, complete with a little flourish at the end, a fine testament to Roy's mastery of the studio.

'All the Way Over The Hill' / 'Irish Loafer (And His Hen)'

The first medley on the album starts with a more straight forward Roy rocker, deploying his usual tricks of great vocals (and Beach Boy harmonies)and a few folk twists. It has a more laid back, soft rock vein than he'd done recently in The Move, and this is another one of his story songs. He sings of unrequited love before his acoustic guitar takes over with some great solo work, and one of his intricate and magnificent sitar/cello solos. He is still using every instrument in his armoury on this one, but it's used sparingly to create intricate and clever sounds. The opening song fades out and launches into the kind of folk jig that either Steeleye Span or Fairport Convention would have been happy with.

'Miss Clarke And The Computer'

This is one of the oddest songs on the album, and one that was very modern for its day. This acoustic and effect-laden piece, with Roy's vocals heavily treated, is all about an office worker's computer falling in love with her. The song takes a very classical guitar piece and adds the treated vocals to provide an interesting and alternative juxtaposition. The traditional musical arrangements, the vocals and the end with its delicate and soft solo, make this one of the most innovative tracks on this album. Again, it displays Roy's knack of being able to make something that was quite technically challenging in the studio sound so simple and work so effectively on the album itself. Who doesn't feel sad for the computer begging Miss Clarke not to reject him?

'When Gran'ma Plays The Banjo'
Released as a single in 1972 b/w 'Wake Up'
Highest UK Chart position: Did Not Chart

This is straight from the Appalachian Deep South, where Roy puts on an American voice in a foot-stomping, hat flinging piece, a story about Gran'ma being one of the best banjo players around. Roy gets to go nuts on his latest musical acquisition, and there's plenty of dextrous and intricate banjo playing. It does sound like Roy is having a lot of fun on this, channelling the American south via the West Midlands. That said, picking this as the lead single makes you wonder what the record label were thinking! It must have really confused everybody.

'Rock Medley – Rockin' Shoes / She's Too Good For Me / Locomotive'
Roy is a massive fan of the Everly Brothers and 1950s rock, and it shows on this medley kicking off with some fantastic slide guitar, an Elvis-style vocal and some proper foot-tapping old school 1950s rock and blues that leads into a recycled Move number 'She's Too Good For Me, where, to make it work, Roy records it as an Everly Brothers-style song. The harmonies are sublime, the backing is as authentic as can be, and it works a lot better here, now it's been reinterpreted via late 1950s American rock. In the full version, it's one of the great lost songs by The Move and it's a shame that they didn't quite take this approach first time out. This is one of the most impressive parts on this album, and Roy's vocals hit the spot every time, as he's got the phrasing spot on to evoke that era. This leads into the brass-driven 'Locomotive', with a cheeky little brass and guitar riff that Roy would return to later with *Wizzard Brew*

Mid-70s Solo Singles
'Forever' b/w 'Music to Commit Suicide By'
Written and produced by Roy Wood
Released 16 November 1973 on Harvest
Highest UK Chart position: 8
Currently available on *Roy Wood The Wizzard – Greatest Hits and More*
Harvest/Parlophone released 2006

'Forever' was a UK top ten solo single for Roy, issued in the same year as Wizzard's 'I Wish it Could Be Christmas Every Day'. It sees him taking his love of music by bands like The Beach Boys and Neil Sedaka, and turning it into a wonderful homage to that mid 60's sound, complete with charming piano, harmony vocals and a bouncing beat. It's another one of Roy's classic pop songs, following themes and imagery that he had honed throughout Wizzard's run of hits throughout 1973. This was his 5th top twenty single during the year, as a solo artist and with Wizzard, which was a run he hadn't managed with The Move, and made his chart run in 1972/1973 with The Move, ELO, Wizzard and solo a phenomenal feat.

The record-buying public in those dim, dismal days of three day weeks, strikes and a hamstrung Conservative Government needed something to liven things up, and these were the glory days for Glam, where pop and rock music was pure escapism, and the gaiety on *TOTP* was in direct contrast to the beige and browns of British Leyland and British life.

If Roy could be said to have done anything, his music made this era a lot brighter and much more colourful.

The flipside has a wonderfully cheerful title and follows Roy's fairly common practice of putting instrumentals on the flip side of his singles. With it's easy-listening-style intro, the track begins as a lovely guitar piece, but it turns into something altogether darker, with its massed ranks of multi-tracked oboes and cellos, so that it becomes the darker evil twin of 'The Battle for Marston Moor' from the debut ELO album. The thundering drums, discordant crashes and clashing instruments, not to mention the clash of styles give an indication here as to where Roy may have taken things had he stayed within ELO.

'Goin' Down the Road' b/w 'The Premium Bond Theme'
Written and produced by Roy Wood
Released on Harvest 7 June 1974
Chart position: UK: 13
Currently available on *Roy The Wizzard- Greatest Hits and More*, released 2006

Roy's only solo single of 1974 is a real move away from his sound of 1973, and an absolute wonderful slice of experimental songwriting. It was his last Harvest single after their successful partnership from 1970. It contains lyrics full of social commentary and contains a mix of a traditional-style folk-rock (in the style of Fairport or Steeleye Span) mixed with the percussive drum and bass more traditionally found backing Bob Marley and the Wailers. Roy sings in a more natural voice on this track, in which he almost speaks, a completely different vocal style to one he'd used previously, and this helps mix the genres up beautifully. Birmingham also had a vibrant folk scene and the biggest folk band of the era – The Ian Campbell folk group – were Birmingham based. Ian's son's Duncan and Ali founded UB40, who brought smooth English reggae to the masses in the 1980s. The Campbells also introduced Fairport Convention's Dave Pegg and Dave Swarbrick to the group. As ever, mixing genres and crossing styles shows how ahead of his time, Roy was. It contains some wonderful crunchy guitar, sparse saxes and the shuffling percussion of reggae. This is mixed with pipes and a military band sound in a fascinating mash-up. Roy's new instrument of choice, the bagpipes (which are all over the next solo album, *Mustard*) are very much in evidence.

This is probably one of the biggest shifts in songwriting style Roy ever made, and while it just missed the top ten, it's still a great track, making the top twenty. Eight years after his first hit single with The Move, it showed that he was still happy to innovate.

The flipside is another one of Roy's instrumental pieces, and with its big strings and ominous chords, it comes as no surprise that this is a homage to the James Bond theme, and the big dramatic Bond songs of this era, showing Roy in yet another different light as a composer. Mixing his trademark saxes and other brasses, this is a dynamic and quite effective homage with plenty of nods to the Bond tune, bringing the theme to mind, without ever actually plagiarising it, showing the depth of skill and class Roy brings to his recordings, even if this was just for a B-side.

'Oh, What A Shame' b/w 'Bengal Jig'
Released on Jet Records in May 1975
Chart position: UK: 13
Currently unavailable

Roy's first single of 1975, and first on the Jet label, followed the demise of Wizzard. It began a new contract for his solo work and followed the pattern of the previous single by being a solid top twenty hit without quite bouncing into the top ten. It's a bouncing, rock-driven piece, with some fabulous honking sax, a great guitar break, and the first appearance of the lyrical motif 'back on the road again'. There's a wonderful Beach Boys vocal homage and overall it is more reminiscent of the Wizzard than his previous single, 'Goin' Down the Road'.

The B-side see's Roy taking two unlikely musical bedfellows and throwing them together, the sitar and the bagpipes. It is, as its name suggests, a Scottish-style jig reminiscent of the sort of high-speed instrumental whirls that fellow Birmingham-based musician Dave Swarbrick was concocting with folk-rock behemoths Fairport Convention. The sitar was something Roy used to great effect in The Move, and the bagpipes were a new toy. So why not throw them both together in a style not unlike 'Goin' Down the Road'? It's not going to top the list of Roy Wood compositions, but it shows Roy's creative side and his sense of fun, plus it follows on the habit of having a good time with his B-Sides that he started with Wizzard.

Mustard (album)

Written, arranged and produced by Roy Wood
Personnel:
All instruments and voices by Roy Wood
Phil Everly: guest vocals on 'Get on Down Home'
Annie Haslam: guest vocals on 'The Rain Came Down'
Engineers at De Lane Les: Dick Plant, Mike Pela, Roy Wood.
Engineers at Phonogram: Pete Oliff, Roger Wake, Steve Brown.
Released on Jet Records November 1975
Chart Position: did not chart
Current edition: Esoteric 2019

Roy's second solo album, released after two highly regarded Wizzard records, is again a solo album in the truest sense. He had stepped back from being the bandleader, to be the whole band. With the help from a couple of high calibre guests in Annie Haslam and Phil Everly, Roy played everything else on here and the album bridges the gap between his early 1970s sound and the more mature jazz-inspired style that his later albums would embrace. It's certainly, more widescreen in sound than *Boulders*, featuring two singles which didn't grace the charts, and when the album itself was released in 1975, just before Christmas, it got lost in the festive flurry of 'Best Of' compilations. The switch from EMI to Jet records may not have helped, as Jet were an independent label and did not have the marketing clout of EMI. He was also stuck in a complicated business situation which is alluded to in the sleeve notes for the deleted Edsel reissue of the album from 1999. In the interview, Alan Robinson quotes from a contemporary interview with Roy in which he explained that he was contracted, at one point, to both Harvest and Warners, which meant he had to record material for both.

This is why there was a glut of solo singles on EMI, running alongside his work with Wizzard and if you look at all the material he released in the three years from leaving ELO, he released two solo albums, two Wizzard albums and a host of singles. It was a work rate that was hard to keep up, and it's no wonder that he wasn't so productive in the latter part of the 1970s. But what a period of music it was, covering the whole spectrum of sounds and styles across the 1970s, charting the evolution of his own style from psych, to prog, to rock, through glam and while often overlooked, *Mustard* is a perfect bookend to this creative period. In 1999 Edsel/Demon remastered and reissued both *Eddie and the Falcons* and *Mustard*, as well as curating the first release of the lost Wizzard album *Main Street*. With superb sleeve notes and bonus tracks, they collected the full recorded output from this period. Thankfully, with the Edsel versions long out of print, the album was reissued by Esoteric in 2019.

It has a wonderful cartoon cover drawn by Roy of him escaping from a pot of mustard, playing the bagpipes, and why not? Wizzard member Rick Price took all the pictures that adorn the inner sleeve, with Wood playing a variety of instruments.

Sonically, this is an evolution of the *Boulders* sound and has plenty of nods to his work with Wizzard. While Boulders has that wonderful, intimate charm, *Mustard* is a real contrast, with a far broader canvas. Roy took full advantage of the studios to create something that has a lot of character and a lot of clever production techniques, brilliant songwriting and an expansive sound palette. These factors make *Mustard* my favourite Roy Wood solo album.

'Mustard'

Showing Roy's affection for different styles and genres, the opening shot on this record, complete with scratched record effect, is a fantastic Andrews Sisters pastiche, with some rather fine doo-wop, 1940s style singing and harmony effects, all created by Roy at play in the studio. With everything played on the album by him, he stretches the limits of what the studio can do, and this is an affectionate pastiche of those close vocal group sounds, in the same way that he paid homage to English music hall in tracks like 'My Marge' and 'The Duke Of Edinburgh's Lettuce'. While he is a fine songwriter, there is also a sense of fun on a lot of his records, a facet of music that musicians who take themselves a tad more seriously tend to forget.

'Any Old Time Will Do'

With its piano-driven riff and sax, this is peerless Wood. It's got a wonderful mid-1970s singer/songwriter vibe to it. It's an honest love song and Wood is on fine vocal form. The drumming – also by Wood – is fantastic, propelling the song along at a great pace. The way he blends the guitars, the pianos, the backing vocals and charming lyrics, make this a lost classic. It's also a shame that when this was released as a single the following year, it disappeared without a trace, with Wood's own blend of pop and rock falling out of favour with the music-buying public increasingly turning towards other musical styles.

'The Rain Came Down On Everything'

Roy has a wonderful way of using rain as a metaphor throughout his songwriting and the haunting, string-powered sound of this track, complete with vocals from Annie Haslam, and Roy delivering one of the most affecting and moving vocal performances of his career, make this a truly beautiful song. The orchestration here is dense and lush, and to make it sound the way a real orchestra would do, the story has it that Roy had seats placed throughout the studio where each individual member of the orchestra would have sat. He then played the relevant instrument in that seat to build up the sound and create the actual orchestra effect. This is part of what makes this song so sublime, as the orchestral power underscores the emotion in Roy's voice, enhancing what is already one of his finest pieces of songwriting. It has storm and rain effects panning across the channels, making the most of the stereo sound, recalling the production on 'Flowers in the Rain'. Indeed, the arrangement is in the vein of some classic big ballads, resplendent with pizzicato strings to symbolise the rain, making this one of the 'big' songs on this record.

'You Sure Got It Now'

There is a sudden change in mood and this song starts off again with an Andrews Sisters vibe, complete with jazzy piano and treated vocal effects. This song drifts and flows, as the boogie piano and harmonica breaks build and speed up as the song kicks into gear, delivering another faux Elvis, in the style of 'California Man'. A big beat kicks in, as he pulls off a brilliant trick, blues-ing it right up with some powerful, driving funk. It's amazing how many of Roy's songs are so funky – he can pull off big bass funk sounds with aplomb, and the treated vocals make him sound like a cross between Rod Stewart and Tina Turner. He pulls out his trusty guitar for a blinding solo to finish this great track off.

'Why Does A Pretty Girl Sing Those Sad Songs?'

With some great vocal harmonies, something Wood has always been a master of, this draws influence from The Beach Boys, who Roy had worked with the previous year when Wizzard were touring the US and this is a fine slice of 'California dreaming', filtered through Roy's unique songwriting vision. It is one track that could definitely have fitted the last Wizzard album, as well as bringing to mind the whole rock n' roll revival sound that made the last few Move singles so good. This scattergun approach of different genres hopping and bouncing around on the same record, could, in lesser hands, sound like a complete hotchpotch, but in skilled fingers like Roy's, there is beautiful synchronicity to the album, and it flows beautifully.

'The Song'

Quite a few of the songs on here stretch out, giving them time to build and grow, and three of them are over six minutes long. This is one of them, with a vocal performance full of the fragility and emotion that Roy brought to bear on 'Whisper In The Night', as his delicate piano work underpins another piece of classic Wood. Mixing classical motifs and rock sounds, once again he references ideas that he first floated in the Electric Light Orchestra, but instead of the dense, heavy sound of the cellos, this is far more pared back, building up slowly and delicately, with trumpet flourishes, and featuring a delicate string and piano piece that is more *BBC Proms* than

Top of the Pops. Roy is in a far more wistful and melancholic mood here as a songwriter.

The instrumental passage, with its grace and subtlety, is pure crossover perfection, reminiscent of the delicate orchestrations of Jon Lord, and show a totally different side to Roy as a composer and writer. This sort of arrangement is where his solo albums tend to stand out, in that he has the freedom to write great songs and not worry about having to fit them to a genre, and this is just lovely.

'Look Thru' The Eyes Of A Fool'
The one track that could have dropped off any Wizzard album, this was the lead single from the album released in November in 1975, and like the rest of the record and its associated singles, it failed to chart. Yet this has a peppy, bouncing rhythm, resplendent with wonderful sax breaks, terrific piano and pounding drums that are in the same vein as 'Ballpark Incident', or 'See My Baby Jive'. This is a fantastic track, and Roy's vocals are on fine form. It is another one of his 'teenage' love songs, with some great lyrics and a rocking beat. It seems like a perfect choice of single, following on from previous records, and it still baffles me to this day why this wasn't a hit.

'Interlude'
Shorter even than the title track, 'Interlude' is exactly as it suggests, taking the bagpipes that Roy is playing on the cover and treated vocal harmonies and military percussion, it is a Scottish lament, played and performed brilliantly by Roy. If you love those big moments when the pipes kick in as I do, the way he produces it and builds up it, even in the shortest breath, is wonderfully stirring stuff. If of course, you don't like bagpipes, it only lasts one minute 24 seconds and you can soon move onto the last track on the album.

'Get on Down Home'
As we've already seen, Roy has had a habit of closing albums with long tracks, almost as a big old musical finale (see 'Feel Too Good' from *Looking On*, or 'Wear A Fast Gun' from *Wizzard Brew*), and this one, complete with Phil Everly on vocals in the middle, is no exception. Clocking in at over seven minutes it's the daddy of this album. It's full of honking sax, riffing guitars and big meaty beats, alongside textured vocals, and a groovy vibe. The distinctive vocals of Phil Everly provide a wonderful counterpoint to Roy's, and with its metronomic beat, not to mention the way it builds and grows, it reminds me very much of 'Feel Too Good', but filtered through the Wizzard machine. There are plenty of meaty, almost heavy metal riffs from Roy, and the way he weaves his vocals and Phil's together creates quite a track.

There is even a sighting of that rare beast, a Roy Wood drum solo. That may feel a little over the top these days, but they were ubiquitous in the 1970s, and if it's good enough for John Bonham, it's good enough for Roy. The way he weaves it around in the song creates chaos like that of Zep's 'Whole Lotta Love', before the beat kicks back in and finishes off with some astounding guitar work.

Singles
'Look Thru' The Eyes of a Fool' b/w 'Strider'
Written and produced by Roy Wood
Released on Jet Records in November 1975
Chart position: didn't chart.

'Strider' is an interesting and eclectic instrumental B-Side, mixing detuned piano, jazz-style sax riffery and some fantastic stereo effects with synths, driving guitar and Wood's use of his musical toybox. It's a display of Roy's mastery of many different instruments, production techniques, and virtuosity and it also signposts the improvisational, free form jazz stylings that Roy was interested in at the time, and keen to explore further. The track was also included on the *Mustard* re-issue.

'Any Old Time Will Do' b/w 'The Rain Came Down on Everything'
Written, produced and performed by Roy Wood
Released on Jet Records May 1976
Both tracks from the album *Mustard*
Chart position: didn't chart

These two album tracks were paired as single and were again unsuccessful in reaching the charts.

On the Road Again (album)
Written and produced by Roy Wood
Personnel:
Roy Wood, vocals, drums, saxes, celli, electric bass, electric guitar, percussion, acoustic guitars, bongos, sitar, slide guitar, mandolin, tuba, vibes, bagpipes, clarinet, violin, bass clarinet, string bass, military percussion.
Recorded at Rockfield Studios (Monmouth, DJM (London) Utopia Studios (London) The Music Centre (Wembley) Air (London) Lee Sound Studios (Pelsall)
Originally released in August 1979
Warner Bros Records (US/Germany/Netherlands only)
Availability: Currently only available in *Roy Wood – The Original Album Series*
Parlophone/Warner Brothers 2014

Astonishingly, Roy's third solo album and his last of the 1970s was never even released in the UK when first issued, only seeing the light of day in the US, Germany and the Netherlands. This was at the insistence of Mo Ostin, the boss at Warner Brothers. However, this is more of a group effort than any of Roy's previous solo albums and has a fantastic guest list of artists and some great tracks, all virtually unknown. A CD reissue licensed from Warner Bros through their third party Wounded Bird record label, snuck out in 2007 (alongside *Super Active Wizzo*) and is no longer available. The only other way to get this album is either second hand or digitally.

This album itself is very reminiscent of *Message from the Country* in terms of style and context, being the follow up to the more complex and longer *Super Active Wizzo* and it sees Roy focusing on shorter songs. However, as we'll see, just because the songs are shorter doesn't mean they are ant less complex. It mixes all of the different styles Wood had worked on with throughout the 1970s and it's a superb collection of material. Criminally, it has yet to receive the reissue treatment. It's long overdue.

'(We're) On The Road Again'
Track credits: Paul Robbins: Roland J4 synthesiser, Clavinet, percussion, backing vocals and Andy Fairweather-Low: backing vocals.

By 1979, disco was everywhere and many musicians were taking disco elements and fusing them into their own music (Eg. The Electric Light Orchestra's 1979 album *Discovery*! Disco? Very!). Many argue that disco and not punk was the driving musical genres of the late 1970s and it was certainly more commercially successful. Late 1970s teenagers preferred to go out and dance rather than listen to complex music. Throughout this album, there are hints of that disco element.

It's there in the pulsating bassline and driving riff on this titular track, for instance. Of course, Roy has always had an element of funk and soul in his musical bag; The Move's 'Feel Too Good', for instance, is a pure slice of late 1960s soul. It's inevitable that, as a songwriter, Roy would pick up on these prevailing trends. The song blends those styles in with his rockier style of writing, and it contains a pulsating synth that bubbles under the arrangement, while the cellos add a touch of that old school Move vibe.

The lyrics add a slightly darker undertone as well, suggesting that the protagonist's favourite band are the highlight of his week, with lyrics like 'we'll make ya feel alright, but after Saturday night, you're back on the dole again' you can't help but remember this is a snapshot of Britain in summer of 1979. The nation was polarized, and things weren't getting better. The chorus, sung by Roy with Paul Robbins and Andy Fairweather-Low, gives the track some power and with more collaborators in place, this feels like a genuine band song, complete with some sublime sax and synth soloing courtesy of Wood and Robbins. This musical collaboration is one that was carried over from the Wizzo band and it helps add a sense of continuity to the record.

The song was also released as a single in the UK, backed with the then-unreleased 'Saxmaniax', which later emerged on the *Main Street* album – and is covered elsewhere.

'Wings Over the Sea'

Track credits: John Bonham: drums, Paul Robbins: piano, electric 12 string guitar, backing vocals. Billy Paul: Alto Sax, Pete Mackie: bass and backing vocals, Carl Wayne: backing vocals

Roy pulled together a fantastic guest list of collaborators for this album, with fellow Wizzo band stalwarts Paul Robbins and Billy Paul in the band while former Wizzard member Charlie Grima also makes an appearance. However, the biggest name on this album (after Wood of course) is an old friend – the pretty well known Led Zeppelin drummer John 'Bonzo' Bonham. Bonham, of course, was invited to join The Move and this track sees him reunited not only with Wood, but also Roy's former Move compadre Carl Wayne, who adds vocals to this track.

This acoustic and sax driven song shows Roy's folkier side and is reminiscent of the sound of *Boulders*. It's one of Roy's big ballads, and features some of his more wistful imagery, using the sort of wordplay and scene-setting familiar in songs like 'Flowers in the Rain' for instance. Indeed, the use of the sitar by Wood does suggest some of his earlier works, while the sax of Billy Paul works wonderfully well with the vocal harmonies. Meanwhile, the drumming from John Bonham is tastefully subtle, a reminder, if any were needed, that he was more than just a powerhouse drummer. This and the opener make a remarkably strong start for the album.

'Keep Your Hands on the Wheel'

Track credits: John Bonham: drums, Paul Robbins: piano, electric 12 string guitar, backing vocals, Billy Paul: Alto Sax, Pete Mackie: bass and backing vocals, Carl Wayne: backing vocals

The other single from the album, backed with 'Giant Footsteps' taken from *Super Active Wizzo*, is one of Wood's rockier tracks. If disco had helped shape one part of the late 1970s sound, the other was a return to the roots of rock and roll. The movie *Grease* had recently become successful, and the late 1950s early 1960s was being seen, once again, as a golden age of music. Wood had already visited this era in the early 1970s with The Move's last run of chart success and followed that through with the success of the early Wizzard tracks like 'Ballpark Incident', 'Angel Fingers' and 'See My Baby Jive'.

He returns to old glories on this track, with the same musicians as on 'Wings Over The Sea' and this sense of cohesion is what keeps this album focused. This track is a great homage to that sound, mixing up a trademark Wood sitar solo, some Beach Boy style harmonies and a great, driving, laid-back rock and roll vibe. Had this been released in 1974, it would have been a huge hit. However, by 1979, certain tastemakers had unfortunately moved on, leaving Roy behind, which was an absolute tragedy.

'Colourful Lady'

Track credits: Pete Mackie: lead vocals, electric rhythm guitar, Paul Robbins: piano, electric 12 string guitar, backing vocals Charlie Grima: congas

One of the reasons that this album is reminiscent of *Message from the Country*, is because of the collaboration between Roy Wood and Paul Robbins who appears on all the tracks. It takes a lot of its musical cues from its predecessor *Super Active Wizzo* but in a shorter, more focussed way. This track, featuring Wood and Robbins sharing the vocal duties, also has some incredibly funky solos from both of them. It is in the jazz-rock vein of the previous album, which showed where Wood's tastes lay at the time and is reminiscent of bands like Quantum Jump and Colosseum II, that blended rock and jazz successfully. But this takes the longer form sound of *Super Active Wizzo* and compresses it to single length. The way the guitars duel and the funky beats provided by former Wizzard man Charlie Grima, mark this out as one of the stand out tracks on the album. It is a superb slice of contemporary jazz-rock, with much to say, as well as showing how versatile a writer Roy was. Unfortunately, a talent as diverse as Roy's has always been eclectic (you only need to look at the genres he covered on *Boulders* to see that) and the mainstream media tend to want to put people in a little box, so when Roy stretched his talents and headed off into other songwriting arenas, he didn't get the acclaim he deserved. This is one of those songs. It's a wonderful feast, in which the musicians find a real groove and spur each other on and in Robbins, Roy found a musical collaborator that was the equal of his partnership with Jeff Lynne in The Move.

'Road Rocket'

Track credits: Paul Robbins: piano and backing vocals, Pete Mackie: bass, backing vocal, motorbike

This track is straight out of the songwriting book that brought us 'When Alice Comes Back to the Farm' and 'California Man'. Indeed, Robbins does a fantastic Jerry Lee Lewis impression on the piano, while Wood sings about how his mother ditched the housework for rock and roll. The honking sax and piano-driven rock on this track could have fallen off any of his albums from the early 1970s and, once again, it's such a shame that this was never a hit. The album is chock full of some fantastic tunes that showed that Roy had lost none of his skill or style and the way he bounces between genres on the songs is remarkable. Yet they retain that unique Roy Wood style and identity.

'Backtown Sinner'

Track credits: Paul Robbins: electric guitar, backing vocals Pete Mackie: bass

Opening with some wonderful cello and strings, the guitar then kicks in and this starts what would have been side two on vinyl. It calls on sounds and styles from throughout Roy's career. For instance, the debut ELO album provides tone of the strings, the saxes are from Wizzard, the sublime vocal harmonies are straight from The Move and there are some great vocals from Roy. The title itself references lyrics from the hard rocker 'Rock Down Low' on Boulders. The song itself is a little bit sleazy in the style of old school rock and roll, while Wood finds some wonderfully inventive rhymes from the word 'sinner', including 'ginner', 'winner' and the memorable 'I'll eat you for dinner'. The concept of Roy as some sort of rock and roll lothario is hard to imagine, but otherwise, it's a wonderfully funky opener to side two.

'Jimmy Lad'

Track credits: Paul Robbins: acoustic guitar, recorders, backing vocals, Pete Mackie: bass and backing vocals

Roy has always liked his bagpipes and has a knack for writing an excellent folk song, and with the recorders on this track, this suggests some of the more mellow moments from *Message from the Country*. Roy throws everything into this Scottish-style song, with some sublime slide guitar work. Roy here pens a traditional style lament, showing how sublime his musical knowledge and skills are, while the switch from the vocals and guitar to the bagpipe and marching band section is well-managed, turning the lament into a full march. Then it's more vocal harmonies and the cello sound that Wood perfected in the early 1970s. The percussion work here is sublime, and if you like bagpipes and the way Roy can make them soar, then you'll love this track. Some might think this track a bit slight or an odd musical sidestep for the album. But to me, it's great and so much better than McCartney's 'Mull of Kintyre', against which this track inevitably gets compared.

'Dancin' At The Rainbows End'

Track credits: Paul Robbins: guitar, 12 string guitar and backing vocals, Charlie Grima: congas, Dave Donovan: drums, Annie Haslam and Dick Plant backing vocals

This is another funky disco-lite track, with some more of Wood's fairy tale imagery, mixing some wonderfully evocative lyrics, with a great vocal. Wizzo's Dave Donovan provides the smooth, funky drumming, while Charlie Grima adds flair with his congas, while the main riff on this song is provided by Wood's wonderful sax. There is also some sublime guitar work by Paul Robbins, and again this shows how his collaborative work with Wood really brings this album to life. Wood, as ever, provides a lot of musical input given the variety of instruments he can (and does) play, but it's clear that working with other musicians to help with the heavy lifting always raises his game, and it's easy to tell that throughout this record he and Robbins were bouncing off each other. Renaissance vocalist Annie Haslam adds her unique backing vocals to this track. This is another one of those songs on which Roy manages to blend his rock style with that of the Wizzo band, in a contemporary slice of polished late 1970s pop. He manages to fit a lot of musical chops into just over three minutes of music. Indeed, condensing the style and charm of *Super Active Wizzo* into a pop song is no mean feat, but one which he does here with aplomb and style. His voice is in fine form here, as his funky sax work, and it lifts the song considerably.

'Another Night'
Track credits: Paul Robbins: piano and backing vocals, Pete Mackie: bass and backing vocals, Billy Paul alto sax and backing vocals, Charlie Grima: congas

This is another jazz-flavoured track, foreshadowing Roy's next album with its subject matter and is another song on this album that mixes metaphors around love and vehicles. It has some great, driving guitar work from Roy and some more of the lush vocal harmonies that are all over this album. Paul Robbins piano work helps this smooth track, as Roy sings about trying to get the girl. This is a theme that is recurrent throughout this album, and there is some great conga work from Charlie Grima, boosted by that ubiquitous sax. The band is funky and tight, Billy Paul's sax and Pete Mackie's bass adding some smooth funk fluidity, while Roy's stabbing guitar work is fantastic, as he blends rock and jazz into a cracking little tune. It ends with a wonderful shuffle and doo-wop finish, rather than fading, which rounds the track off nicely.

'Way Beyond the Rain'
Track credits: Paul Robbins: piano, Moog, backing vocals, Pete Mackie: bass and backing vocals, Annie Haslam: backing vocals

I have often mentioned Roy's love of 'big' tracks – songs that define the record they are on and mark the stand out performances on various albums. Despite the huge musical variation on display on this record, nothing quite prepares you for the majesty and beauty of this closing track. It should end up in any top ten of Roy Wood compositions and is one of the most hauntingly beautiful songs that Roy has crafted. It has a wonderful vocal from Roy bringing 'Blackberry Way' to mind, and lyrics that are simple yet effective. Drenched in perfect, lush strings, and with backing vocals again from Annie Haslam (as well as Roy, Paul Robbins and Pete Mackie) it also contains superbly effective multi-tracked cellos, sax and guitar in its middle section.

Roy's soaring vocals build huge amounts of emotion as the string-powered counterpoint builds to a climax. This is 'Queen Of The Hours' in widescreen. Indeed, it feels like the culmination of Roy's vision for The Electric Light Orchestra compared against Jeff Lynne's version and is close in spirit to the debut ELO album. The subtle piano and Moog of Paul Robbins and Pete Mackie's bass underpins the arrangement, while Roy builds a lush, intense sonic tapestry over the top. There's a huge amount going on here and it just tugs at the heartstrings so that it's hard to believe that the track is really only just over five minutes long. It's the perfect way to end a sublime album, and one that really shows the many facets of Roy's songwriting skills.

The Singles 1980-1982

Between 1980 and 1982 Roy released several singles independently and as part of the band Helicopters. All told, there's pretty much an entire album's worth of material.

Luckily, when *Message from the Country*, *Wizzard Brew* and *Boulders* were reissued in 2006, EMI also put out a collection which is still available, called *The Wizzard – Roy Wood,* which collects all the singles, and several B-Sides, by The Move, ELO, Wizzard and the Roy Wood solo singles when he was on the EMI label from 1969-1974 and again from 1980-1982. This collects eight singles previously unreleased on CD and two completely unreleased singles. While some of the material duplicates material found on *Message from the Country* and *Boulders*, it is the only place to find the four Wizzard singles (including 'I Wish it Could Be Christmas Everyday') on CD and at a low price, it is a worthwhile investment.

Roy Wood's Helicopters

Between 1979 and 1982, Roy formed the band Helicopters with Renaissance bassist Jon Camp and touring musicians Paul Robbins (who Roy had collaborated so successfully with as part of the Wizzo Band and throughout the *On the Road Again* era), Robin George, Mike Deacon and Kex Gorin. Two singles were released, but a third one 'Aerial Pictures' b/w 'Airborne' was cancelled and the project fizzled out.

'Rock City' b/w 'Givin' Your Heart Away'

Written and produced by Roy Wood
Released on Cheapskate Records in 1980
Highest UK Chart position: didn't chart
Currently Unavailable but available on YouTube

Starting with a very angular choppy riff and some funky bass, 'Rock City' sees Roy Wood channelling the new wave into his songwriting. Although technically, a band including Jon Camp, on this single Roy (as on Boulder and Mustard) played all the instruments.

Reminiscent of the syncopated sounds of On the Road Again, and featuring a synth solo – probably a first for a Woody single – 'Rock City' updates his Wizzard lyrical themes, although not as substantially as on some of the earlier singles. It does have a catchy chorus and some great production by Roy. Indeed, I would argue that the use of electronic instrumentation works far better on here than on Starting Up and the track returns to familiar territory with a great sax solo at the end. For the first time in his career Roy wasn't signed to a major label, and despite his pedigree, this song 'escaped' rather than being released, and, like all of Roys latter singles, made no impact on the charts.

The flip side, despite having a synth riff throughout, covers far more traditional songwriting ground for Roy and features semi-regular contributor Annie Haslam singing on the chorus. Roy produced the Renaissance vocalists' *Annie In Wonderland* album and was in a relationship with her in the 1970s. It is more firmly rooted in Roy's 'teen ballad' style of writing. A mid-paced rock song about the pitfalls of stepping into a new relationship, it's sound owes a lot to slower tempo tracks like 'Beautiful Daughter', 'Dancin' At The Rainbows End' or 'Any Old Time Will Do') and it does seem to be treading old ground. Despite Annie's vocals and some great guitar from Roy, it's not the finest song he released during this era, and despite some string work that harks back to the ELO album, it's one of those tracks that never really gets going, even though Roy gives his all to his vocals.

'Green Glass Windows' b/w 'The Driving Song'
Written and produced by Roy Wood
Featuring the Kempsey Primary School Choir
Released by EMI on 30 March 1981
Highest UK Chart position: didn't chart
Current availability: currently available on *Roy The Wizzard – Greatest Hits and More*
Harvest/Parlophone, released 2006

This is an absolute lost classic of a Roy Wood track, mixing elements of new wave, synth pop and classic Wood themes. It has a fantastic bass riff and interesting synth fills, also utilising the classic Wood motif of a primary school choir, which worked so well on 'I Wish it Could Be Christmas Everyday' and 'Sing Out The Old'. This mixes Roy's classic sound, including some guitar that could have dropped off any Move album, with some fantastic contemporary songwriting and a mix of synth sounds that works well as a transition between his classic 1970s sound, and the 1980s-style production on *Starting Up*. However, this is more than a transitional piece and a worthy addition to his back catalogue. It also has some fantastic lyrics, reminiscent of his 'adult' fairy tales from The Move, and shows he'd lost none of his finesse and songwriting chops. In fact, the mix of the old and the new works better here than it does on some of the *Starting Up* tracks, feeling more like an organic follow up to *On the Road Again*.

The flipside has more synth and some sampled car sounds. It again foreshadows *Starting Up* and symbolises Roy's latest obsession of cars. It uses his rocking style, updating the 'California Man' template for the 1980s and sees Roy sharing vocal duties with West Midlands legend Noddie Holder. Two West

Midlands legends for the price of one! It's a terrible shame that it was tucked away as a B-Side, at probably the nadir of both of their careers. And yet this has some fantastic guitar work from Roy, great sax work and the way he and Noddy trade vocals is a joy. The Duane Eddy guitar riff mixed with a pounding beat make this a perfect driving song. Cruise the A42 with the window down listening to this slab of retro rock and roll.

'Aerial Pictures' b/w 'Airborne'

Written and produced by Roy Wood
Scheduled for released in 1982 but cancelled
First released on: *Roy Wood The Wizzard – Greatest Hits and More*
Harvest/Parlophone 334 1362 released 2006

Again, this song is very much in the new wave sound, taking Roy's trademark vocals and mixing it with a burbling synth, making it reminiscent of Mike Oldfield disco hit 'Guilty'. Here we have the original, unreleased version of a song that eventually came out as Carl Wayne single in 1982. 'Aerial Pictures' is another 'story' song, marking a subtle shift in his songwriting style, in which the main instrument is the synthesiser and traditional instrumentation takes a back seat. Astonishingly, this languished in the EMI vaults for over 25 years until it made it's debut in 2006 and is another one of those lost classics that prove that Roy hadn't lost his touch with a guitar riff. The way his guitar and synth mix together is joyous.

'Airborne' was the proposed B-Side to 'Aerial Pictures'. It is a wonderful paean to flying, and with its nods to answerphones and flying high, its pre-dates ELO's 'Calling America', with its similar themes, by five years and see's Roy again mixing his guitar with some wonderfully squelchy synth sounds. Taking the 'doo-wop' approach to backing vocals, it mixes his rock and roll ideals with contemporary sounds. With a fantastic vocal and a crunchy riff, this is the wall of sound updated for the 1980s. Mix up the old and bring in the new seemed to be the motto for Roy at the time, and it's such a shame that we didn't get a full album of tracks like this, 'Green Glass Windows' and 'Aerial Pictures', as it could have been a career-defining moment instead of the watered-down sound we got eventually with *Starting Up*.

'Sing Out The Old, Bring In The New' b/w 'Watch This Space'

Written and produced by Roy Wood
Originally released in 1980 on Cheapskate records, reissued in 1985 on Legacy records
Highest UK Chart position: didn't chart
Not currently available

This is an attempt to write another classic Christmas song, complete with Wizzard style saxes, for the new decade. It has some great vocals and lyrics that relate to the season of goodwill. It also has the obligatory children's choir on the chorus (presumably the same choir as on 'Green Glass Windows'), sitar and all the musical elements that Roy threw in the pot to create 'I Wish It Could Be Christmas Every Day'. There are plenty of similarities between both songs; both have catchy choruses, sweet verses about the joys of Christmas and that full-on wall of sound meets falling snow that made the original such a hit.

However, this song totally disappeared without a trace and until the 1985 remixed version appeared on the now sadly deleted *Look Thru' The Eyes of Roy Wood* compilation from 2007, covering the 1974 -1987 period on the Sanctuary label, it remained undiscovered.

It's a good song, but it did seem a bit retro for the time it was made and it is astonishing that 'I Wish it Could Be Christmas Everyday' still sold in decent numbers, yet this clever attempt to follow it up and create a new Christmas single tradition never got the attention it deserved.

It may be because of the death of John Lennon put a dampener on Christmas 1980, so the bouncier style of Christmas song was considered inappropriate at the time. On its reissue in 1985, big Christmas songs like this were on their way out, and it didn't even get a look in compared to the big hitter of the year in the UK, Shakin' Stevens 'Merry Christmas Everyone'. It's ironic that Stevens was successful by playing homage to the old school rock 'n roll that Roy had also done with Wizzard barely a decade earlier, yet with a lot less of the charm than Roy!

The flipside, 'Watch This Space', sees Roy going back to the tradition that started with Wizzard of instrumental B-sides and this is another jazz-influenced piece. This track is almost like a musical pic 'n' mix from Roys career to date, with some of that contemporary disco beat that is all over *On the Road Again*. The guitar riff jumps and flows like some of the mellower Move tracks – with a hint of 'Jumpin' Biz' in there as well – and the sax breaks could have fallen straight off the Wizzo album. For old times sake, there's even a sitar solo in there. As instrumentals go, this is a tremendous mid-paced toe tapper and is one of the stronger b-sides Roy released in this period, showing that he'd lost none of his sense of experimentation and his flair for doing the unexpected on his single releases.

'Down to Zero' b/w 'Olympic Flyer'
Written and produced by Roy Wood
Released on EMI Records EMI5203 in 1981
Chart position: didn't chart
Currently available on: on *Roy The Wizzard- Greatest Hits and More*
Harvest/Parlophone 334 1362 released 2006

'Down To Zero' is a very traditional Roy rocker, although there are hints of synth in here, and it has a great, catchy chorus. It has a nagging riff and some rather more traditional rock instrumentation from Roy, making it a return to his more rock and roll routes than his work with Wizzo. With a powerful bass lane and solos from guitar and synth, Roy puts a lot of instrumentation into what, initially, sounds like a simple rock and roll chant. But instead, it's a lot more sophisticated than that, with plenty of trademark Woodisms throughout, including harmony vocals, catchy lyrics and a great guitar solo. It is such a shame that singles of this calibre simply slipped through the net at the time.

The flipside continues his theme of putting instrumentals on the B-side, and this track has elements of Mike Oldfield in it, mixing a pulsating disco beat while over the top synths and strings take it in turns to repeat the meaty riff. The strings are fantastic, underpinned by the contrasting electronic disco beat, making 'Olympic Flyer' very much a driving song. The way it flits between conventional recording and instrumentation to more electronic and disco flavoured sounds is a great studio trick, showing Roy adapting his style and sound to fit the 1980s, without losing his adventurous spark.

'It's Not Easy' b/w 'Moonriser'
Written and produced by Roy Wood
Released on 29 January 1982 on EMI records EMI5261
Currently available on *Roy The Wizzard – Greatest Hits and More*
Harvest/Parlophone 334 1362 released 2006
Chart position: didn't chart

Opening with a pulsating synth, this song mixes rock and roll with more modern instrumentation. This was the last new single Roy released on EMI. Any update of the last few singles, it features some social commentary from Roy (following on from 'On the Road Again') 'it's not easy living it up when you're living on the rock and roll'. This is a rock and roll song about being on the dole (rock 'n roll is cockney rhyming slang for the dole) and despite the synths, is in every other way a very traditional Roy single. Mixing the shuffling rock and roll beat, with saxes, harmony vocals and rather more traditional guitar work, it's very much in the vein of earlier Wizzard songs.

Tucked away on the B-side, is 'Moonriser', a classic Wood rocker, mixing the 1980s sound of the new wave, with Roy's tale of a girl who likes living on the edge at night. 'Moonriser' has Roy's multi-layered vocals, a memorable chorus, some funky bass and drum work, and sees him utilising his best rock vocals, before unleashing an absolute belter of a guitar solo.

Stripping the music back to the more conventional rock band sound, this has no quirky touches, like cellos or bagpipes. Even brass, which for so long had informed his arrangements, is noticeably absent. But despite this, 'Moonriser' is a superb rock song, mixing Wood's driving rock sound, great vocals and contemporary production techniques, making it another hidden gem.

Starting Up (album)
Written, produced and performed by Roy Wood
Strings arranged by Louis Clark

Strings by the Royal Philharmonic Violins
Engineered by Al McKerchar (Sinewave Studio)
Colin Owen, Terry Rowley (The Old Smithy Studios)
Mixed by: Alan Caves (Abattoir Studios) Dick Plant (track 8 Nivram Studios) and
Tony Tavener (Track 3 Maison Rouge)
Artwork by Delboy
Released on Legacy Records 1987
Chart Position: Did not Chart
Currently availability: Not available in physical form, but widely available to stream
or download

The last studio album Roy has released to date, *Starting Up* is very much of its
time and is a concept album of sorts. Recorded in 1985 and 1986, it has the
oddest cover of Roy's career. He is dressed as a Samurai in this posed photo,
while the backdrop is an incredibly 1980s, stylised cityscape complete with
a red car, the subject of the album and the writing is in a faux Japanese style.
Whether the budget for the record only stretched to the recordings and not
the artwork, it's hard to say, but when you consider that this is the last album
statement from Roy, it is a shame the cover isn't better.

Having gone from an innovative performer and producer throughout the
1960s and 1970s, at this stage in the game, Roy was best-known for the re-
issues of 'I Wish it Could Be Christmas Every Day' (and it's regular appearance
on Christmas compilation TV shows every December). You can't blame him
for this; after the whole 'Flowers in the Rain' debacle where Wood lost all
his songwriting royalties in perpetuity due to cavalier actions of his manager,
it's not hard to fully understand and appreciate exactly why it's good to have
an annual banker coming in from the Performing Rights Society. Everyone
deserves a Christmas bonus.

If this album was meant to act as a comeback record, it was unsuccessful.
Given that it's now over 30 years since Roy released a studio album, it's
frustrating that this is the last thing he put out. As with several of his albums
and songs, it is unavailable on any physical format at the moment, apart from
some dodgy Japanese bootlegs. Ironically, this was the first album by Roy that I
bought back in the early 1990s when buying hard to find albums was a difficult
process, so my nostalgia for the album is also nostalgia for the great days of the
British high street.

But there are moments on this record can compare favourably not only
with *Boulders*, but to the solo albums by Paul McCartney – *McCartney* in
1970, and then *McCartney II* in 1980. All these albums are solo records in the
truest sense of the word, with both Wood and McCartney playing and writing
everything. Indeed, both *Boulders* and *McCartney* were written as their main
groups were dissolving, and both *McCartney II* and *Starting Up* were the first
solo albums for both men in the 1980s and sees them both experimenting with
contemporary electronic sounds with varying degrees of success.

This is an album that you need to live with for a while to tease out its nuances and pick up on some of the more subtle musical undertones and while it's not on a par with albums like *Wizzard Brew* or *On the Road Again*, there's plenty of charm and some really good songs, even if you do have to get over the dated production and rather metronomic and clunky drum machine. Where this album falls down, is on the tracks where Roy is trying to write in the very contemporary way in an attempt to sound mid-1980s. When he does, he sounds like everybody else at the time, while on the songs where he is just being himself, or honing the prevailing sound of the time to fit his songwriting (and not vice versa) then the results are satisfying. There are at least half a dozen songs on the album that are bona fide Wood classics, even if overall it is never going to be celebrated as the greatest Roy Wood album.

At the point I bought it, many held out hope that Roy would get back in the studio and continue recording. But over 30 years later, he has maintained radio silence on the recording front, although Roy and his band still tour – entertaining his public to this day. The edition used to review the album was released in 1993 on the Castle label, and is basic, containing as it does the album, a pretty basic sleeve, and no bonus tracks or sleeve notes. A more comprehensive remaster was last available on Sanctuary Records back in 2007, when they licensed several of Roy's tracks to put together several different compilation albums (including *Lookin' Thru' The Eyes of Roy Wood* and *Outstanding Performer*) however none of these albums are available anymore and so the buyer's only recourse is to either buy second hand or streaming.

In the context of the singles Roy released in the early 1980s on EMI, *Starting Up* makes a lot more sense, as those singles mark the evolution of his sound, mixing as they do his traditional style songwriting and arrangement with the new technology that fully comes to fruition on *Starting Up*. So, the album is best appreciated in context if you listen to the brace of singles on the *Roy Wood The Wizzar*d! compilation, which bridge the gap between *On The Road Again* and *Starting Up*.

'Red Cars Are After Me'

The opening track, with it's honking sax and funk-driven beat, is one of the funkiest things Roy has put to record. The only thing that jars slightly is the programmed drumming, which is a touch too metronomic. Following on from *On the Road Again*, which had a few songs on there about cars, this album is an entire concept piece around the automobile and its role in the world. Containing some of Roy's wonderful guitar work, the song is quite a good opener and Wood's mastery of the sax (amongst all the other instrumentation) and his Duane Eddy-style guitar, mixes the old and the new. He utilises a range of vocal styles from his usual voice to something like Ian Anderson (from Jethro Tull) and this song mixes contemporary mid-1980s electro-pop with a more organic, classic rock sound.

The lyrics – about being stalked by red cars – provide a slice of driving paranoia, mixing sly humour with genuine observations – many us have felt that we are being followed on long journeys.

'Raining In The City'

Returning to one of Roy's favourite themes, this is a song about rain, and the impact it has on people's emotions, (see also 'Flowers In The Rain', 'The Rain Fell Down On Everything' and 'Way Beyond the Rain') making this is a more 'classic' Roy Wood style song. The programmed drums are further down in the mix, as Wood creates his own wall of sound and builds up a classic Roy ballad, as he watches the world go by as people rush through the city in the rain. His well-written lyrics capture the spirit of the city as he mourns the end of a relationship and the classic sax sound and guitar work recall some of Wizzard's more straight forward rock and roll. This was also released as a single in 1986 to promote the album with an instrumental version on the B-side, but like so much of Roy's new material in the 1980s, it also failed to chart.

'Under Fire'

This is one of the more 1980s-style track on here, starting with sampled vocals and more of that metronomic drum beat and the instrumentation here is pretty much entirely synthesised, giving it the same feel of the Jethro Tull album *Under Wraps*. It has some cleverly sampled and treated vocals to create the harmonies, while the main riff is a great chunky synth beast and the production has Wood's voice prominent in the mix as the driving instrument. As Roy harmonises with himself, it creates an intense vocal vibe and features a great guitar solo that rips through the middle of the song.

'Turn Your Body To The Light'

This is another highly synthesised piece, but instead of replacing the traditional instrumentation, the arrangement enhances the songwriting and (despite those 80s drums) this is one of those songs where the electronic sounds, which can sometimes be so cold, actually make the song warmer. Wood's lead vocals are sublime, having lost none of their power and emotion, and they work beautifully in combination with the vocal harmonies. This is a song of love and lust and has some of Roy's finest lead guitar work, mixing the organic and the electronic to give depth to the song. On some tracks, the use of the synthesiser and programmed drumming is over the top, but here Roy's skill as a performer and songwriter pulls it all together and this song should genuinely be recognised as a lost classic.

'Hot Cars'

A mix of show tune and Art of Noise electro pomp, 'Hot Cars' is full of pumping brass, funky bass and a driving, percussive beat, while Wood sings about the 'Hot Cars' making it to Broadway. There are some lovely guitar work and jazzy echoes of albums like *Main Street* and *Super Active Wizzo*. Roy uses the studio to its full potential on here, riffling like Earl Slick and conjuring up a full jazz big band swing sound, just by himself. I wonder if he sat in every different seat in the studio to get the sound right like he did when recording *Mustard*?

'Starting Up'

With a sampled car engine, this is another incredibly mid 80s sound for Wood. A lot of his songs are timeless, but the production roots the songs here them firmly into a particular era, that it's hard to see past. That doesn't detract too much from the songwriting, however, as 'Starting Up' is another Wood rocker, kicking off side two of the album with engine noises and guitar work (like fellow-Midlands musicians Slade's 'Ready To Explode'). Unlike the other arrangements on this album, which are fairly standard, it also features Roy on sitar, adding some exotic textures.

'Keep It Steady'

Again, this track is very much of its time, it's funky and dance-orientated and it has some heavily synthesised breaks, and sampled vocals. This is one track where the synthesised arrangement works less well. It bounces along at a decent pace, but it doesn't bring anything new to the table and sounds like many songs of that era. Roy has always been at his best when bringing something different to his arrangements. Imagine the amazing array of instruments he played on *Looking On*, for instance, or the verve of 'See My Baby Jive'. Here, it sounds like he's trying to be like everyone else and unfortunately, it just doesn't work.

'On Top Of The World'

Then you go from the generic 1980s sound of 'Keep It Steady' to this, a sublime string-laden rocker, full of optimism and power. This is classic Roy Wood, putting his slant on the ELO vision (which, let us not, forget he co-created) of mixing rock music with orchestral sounds. Just to show how interconnected the whole scene was, Roy gets Louis Clark, former musical director with ELO, to score the strings. Provided by the Royal Philharmonic violins, these are the only instruments played on here by any other musicians. The song is another rocker in the style of 'California Man' or 'Keep Your Hands On The Wheel'. It mixes some wonderful Jerry Lee Lewis piano, Roy's triumphant vocals, and a string-driven accompaniment, helping it to rock along wonderfully.

This might have been the big hit from the album, but the song was relegated to the B-side of 'Under Fire'. Indeed, it is clear that this is one of the songs that had been around for a while, first being released in 1985, then placed on this album. It is one of the strongest tracks on the record and one of Roy's great later songs. Indeed, it has a timeless quality and could have slotted onto any of his albums over the past twenty years.

'Ships in the Night'

Doing something ever so slightly different with the percussion makes a massive difference to this closing track and the mesmeric beat is a counterpoint to Roy's impassioned vocals. Indeed, the way the track is built up from its synth, bass and the slightly psychedelic filter recalls the mid-1980s work of John Foxx on albums like *The Golden Section*. This accentuates Roy's guitar work – in fact, due to the sparseness of the instrumentation, and the reliance on electronic sounds like the drum machines, synths and sampling, this album has Roy's guitar work to the fore – and he plays with real power, with a tone more reminiscent of The New Wave Of British Heavy Metal and this mix of organic raw rock and roll with electronic sounds works incredibly well.

Roy's lyrics are pretty good with some fantastically passionate vocal work and a great lyrical theme. However, the closest it gets to the concepts of cars and motoring is during the slightly disconcerting voice over where it talks about 'It feels like we're being taken over by the Japanese', which is sung in a slightly mocking tone.

The Final Single

'123' (Madea, White, Borissof) **b/w 'Oh What A Shame'** (Wood)
Produced and performed by Roy Wood
Released on Jet records in 1987
Chart position: Didn't chart
Current not available

The final single of original material saw Roy return to his mid-70s home at the Jet Records label, which recycled the 1975 top twenty hit single 'Oh What a Shame' as a B-side, and a cover of the 1965 UK number one hit by Len Barry, who co-wrote the song. You could argue that this is Roy going full circle, 21 years since he released his first single, and covering one of the songs that would no doubt have been everywhere in those heady days of the mid-1960s when The Move were hitting their stride and covering Motown and other R 'n B classics. While it is a good cover of the song, with Roy adding his trademark rock vocals and unique style to it, it seems such an anti-climax for him to bow out of recorded music with such a song.

7. Appendix – The Idle Race

Many bands have plenty of potential; great songs, musical talent in abundance and the knack of doing something ever so slightly different to the mainstream and yet they never broke through into the big time, remaining cults. The Idle Race were probably the finest example of this phenomenon. Consider, for instance, that they had Jeff Lynne (pre The Move and ELO) writing the songs and Eddie Offord (famous for his work with Yes and ELP) producing their first singles. They also had fans in The Beatles and Kenny Everett who said in 1968, 'The Idle Race are second only to the Beatles' and yet they never made much of a dent on the charts or into the wider public consciousness.

Musical hot spots were formed in all of the major cities in the UK during the 1960s, and Birmingham was no exception. As well as The Move and The Idle Race, the city also produced Mike Sheridan and the Nightriders, who originally comprised Mike Sheridan, Dave Pritchard, Greg Masters, Roger Spencer and Roy Wood. Roy quickly moved on to The Move, while the departure of Sheridan meant that the remaining trio of Pritchard, Masters and Spencer had to find a new guitarist. First up came Johnny Mann (from Carl Wayne And The Vikings) who then swiftly departed, then, after placing an advert in the local paper the band discovered Jeff Lynne in 1966. A brief single release on Polydor as the Nightriders came to nought, but the band had already started to change direction and changed their name from The Nightriders To The Idyll Race – the dream of perfection. But, as these things do, the name mutated into The Idle Race, with Jeff firmly placed as the frontman. A deal with Polydor ended, but due to the band's connections with Roy Wood, they were introduced to producers Eddie Offord and Gerald Chevin, and after intensive gigging, they signed a deal with Liberty Records.

While working on their debut album and maintaining their heavy touring schedule, they released their debut single in 1967.

The Early Singles
'Here We Go Round The Lemon Tree' (Wood) b/w **'My Fathers Son'** (Pritchard)
Released on Liberty Records September 1967 US / Europe only.
Currently available on ***Back To The Story....,*** Parlophone 2007 and *The Birthday Party* expanded edition, Grapefruit Records 2020
Personnel:
Jeff Lynne: vocals, guitar
Dave Pritchard: guitar, vocals
Greg Masters: bass guitar, vocals
Roger Spencer: drums, vocals

Their close link with fellow Birmingham band The Move led to them recording this cover of the album track 'Here We Go Round the Lemon Tree' one of

Wood's whimsical, almost nursery rhyme-style songs, lifted from The Move's debut album. Slightly heavier and more up-tempo than the version by The Move, it became The Idle Races debut single, and the only cover version recorded during the Jeff Lynne era. This version also added a more psychedelic guitar break, and some impressive military drumming from Spencer. Other than that, there's not much difference between the two – it's more of an evolutionary than a revolutionary cover. As so often happened at the time, the single was all ready to go in the UK and then, as The Move's version became the B-side of their hit 'Flowers in the Rain' and started to gain traction and airplay, the record label took the decision to pull the plug and issue the single over in USA and Europe only. The B-side, a Dave Pritchard original, also sung by Dave, is more reminiscent of the work of The Kinks than their Birmingham compatriots, a heavy backbeat and some great riffing illustrating a song about living up to your parent's reputation. Lynne's often underrated skill as a guitarist is on show here with some great soloing. It's more a blues-rock stomp than a psychedelia freak out.

'Imposters Of Life's Magazine' (Lynne) **b/w 'Sitting In My Tree'** (Lynne)
Liberty LBF 15026 October 1967 (UK Only)
Currently available on *Back To The Story....* Parlophone 2007 and *The Birthday Party* expanded edition Grapefruit Records 2020
Personnel:
Jeff Lynne: vocals, guitar
Dave Pritchard: guitar, vocals
Greg Masters: bass guitar, vocals
Roger Spencer: drums, vocals

This is where it gets interesting. The first UK single for The Idle Race is far more representative of their sound than the cover of a Move song and it's one of the great lost psychedelic singles. 'Imposters' is a Jeff Lynne classic with some fantastic production at work. Produced by Eddie Offord and Gerald Chevin, it highlights some of the techniques that Eddie would use to great effect when working with Yes in the 1970s, and it shows Lynne's lyrical style with lines such as 'touch your friends' girl, will he mind, will his mind will it?'. It could only come from 1967. Fresh, punchy and with amazing guitar duelling from Pritchard and Lynne, the fact that this non-album track was put out as a replacement for the aborted UK issue of 'Here We Go Round the Lemon Tree' at last minute meant it got virtually no promotion, and instead of racing up the charts, passed the mainstream by without even a glance. Only now, looking back at the vibrant Brum scene has its cultural and musical importance been noted. In fact, back in the early 1990s *Mojo* magazine put together a supplement of the best 100 psychedelic tracks and 'Imposters' was rightly lauded as a great example of English psychedelia.

It is backed with the album cut 'Sitting in my Tree'.

'The Skeleton And The Roundabout' (Lynne) b/w 'Knocking Nails Into My House' (Lynne)

Liberty released February 1968 (UK only)
Currently available on *Back to the Story....* Parlophone 2007 and *The Birthday Party* expanded edition Grapefruit Records 2020
Personnel:
Jeff Lynne: vocals, guitar
Dave Pritchard: guitar, vocals
Greg Masters: bass guitar, vocals
Roger Spencer: drums, vocals

The final of three singles issued before their debut album *The Birthday Party* was released in 1968, this UK only single again failed to make much of an impact and paired the album opener with another non-album track. Lynne's 'Knocking Nails Into My House' (later covered by fellow West Midlands band Ambrose Slade on their debut album) is a story of repossession and debt, set to a jaunty, almost musical hall-style theme, complete with comedy 'boing' noises.

The Birthday Party (album)

Released on Liberty Records October 1968 (UK & USA)
Reissued by Parlophone on Ltd edition Gold Vinyl for Record Store Day 2014
Currently available on *Back To The Story....* Parlophone 2007
Deluxe expanded edition available on Grapefruit Records 2020
Personnel: Jeff Lynne: vocals, guitar
Dave Pritchard: guitar, vocals
Greg Masters: bass guitar, vocals
Roger Spencer: drums, vocals
Recorded at Advision Studios London
All songs by Jeff Lynne unless shown
Produced by Eddie Offord and Gerald Chevin.

The band's debut album was released in 1968 in a lavish gatefold sleeve, complete with an invitation to the birthday party on the front, and a 'party' on the inside featuring a cornucopia of contemporary celebrities including The Beatles and pretty much all of the Radio One DJ line up of the day, reproduced faithfully on both the RSD vinyl edition and the Grapefruit remaster. While it was highly acclaimed, it failed to chart in either the UK and USA.

I came into The Idle Race by the back door. I was a massive Beatles fan and as a natural completist, when I discovered ELO, I then ended up working my way backwards and discovered The Move, before landing on The Idle Race. Due to their lack of commercial success, the only previous reissues of their albums had been somewhere in the mid-1970s to capitalise on the success of ELO in the USA. The chances of finding their albums second hand weren't great. But in 1996 I discovered *Back to the Story*, the double-disc complete Idle Race collection, comprising all three albums, all the singles and the B-sides and a couple of bonus tracks. I really wasn't sure what to expect, as having heard Jeff's work with The Move, it's easy to work out how this dovetails in with the starting point of ELO. The Idle Race, however, was completely different.

In 2020, the Grapefruit label reissued *The Birthday Party* in a deluxe double edition set which includes the stereo album newly remastered, the non-album singles and previously released contemporary outtakes that are on *Back to the Story*. The Grapefruit remaster also includes on disc one, for the first time on CD, the original mono-mix of *The Birthday Party* and while a lot of the songs have minor differences, I will mention these where significant.

At only just over 30 minutes long, this is hardly a mammoth album time-wise, but in terms of its contents, The Idle Race, Jeff Lynne and the production team have put everything they had into this album. And, by and large, it works.

'Skelton And The Roundabout'
The album starts with this music hall-style, nightmarish psychedelic track about a fairground operator who has a roundabout that no-one uses, and by winding the wheels, he becomes thinner and thinner until he becomes the titular skeleton. It is not an average pop song, but then, this was the late 1960s and, as Jeff later said in an interview for *Prog* magazine, he was influenced by his parent's record collection of music hall songs, something which shows throughout this album. Many of the songs are first-person narratives, while many of the characters sit on the periphery of the norm. This is a theme that Jeff would revisit later in his career on ELO tracks like 'Nellie Takes Her Bow', 'Mr Radio' and 'The Diary of Horace Wimp'. It's this juxtaposition of slightly absurd or sad characters or situations, mixed with music hall tunes or rock and roll that make this album so striking, in the manner that later artists like the Beautiful South would do. Of all the tracks on the album, this is one with the biggest difference between the stereo and mono mix, giving the listener extra lyrics fleshing out the titular character's back story.

'Happy Birthday' (Mildred J. Hill & Patti S. Hill) / 'The Birthday Party'
Tracks two and three segue nicely into each other, the first being a mournful downbeat version of the traditional 'Happy Birthday' song, played here at a funereal pace rather than with the usually enforced jollity, leading into a sad story about a girl on the periphery who organised a birthday party that no-one came to. Opening with a Lynne trademark of strings and vocals, the song feels almost like a traditional ballad, with harmony vocals and descending strings mixing with guitars and effects. Female characters on the edge of society, lonely and trying to fit in, was a theme Jeff often revisited and while this sad song of a birthday party that no-one attended doesn't have a happy ending, it's tone – a mini-symphony – signposts a future direction for him.

'I Like My Toys'

This is a jaunty little song with jangling guitar, plus driving drum and bass, and tells the story of a young man living at home with his parents and obsessed with his collection of toys.

It has a pulsating, military beat and a male choir intoning the boy's mother's threats in a style that almost sounds like a Welsh male voice choir. A refrain of 'I say that I'm not well' and other lyrics about heading to the stars suggest there is something more going on here than we're told. Indeed, most of the tracks on this album are snapshots or vignettes. This whole album could be construed as a look at twelve different lives and windows that we get a sneaky peek into with no back story, and no context, so we're left to think about these characters and guess what the rest of their stories might be. It's great, intelligent pop.

'Morning Sunshine'

This is a slower-tempo piece with some tribal drumming, and a wonderfully emotive guitar solo, from a trick of Jeff's to use a violin bow on his guitar – a sound that he would replicate during the ELO days. It's easy, in hindsight, to spotlight what parts of these songs Jeff took with him, first to The Move and then onto the ELO set up, but this could easily have slipped into any ELO album from the early 70s, with Jeff's trademark vocals prominent. This isn't the Jeff Lynne show, however, The Idle Race were very much a band, albeit one like The Move with a recognised songwriter, but the musical talents of Roger Spencer on drums and Greg Masters on bass provide the backbeat, allowing Jeff Lynne and Dave Pritchard to duel on guitar, while harmony vocals are also a trademark of the band and one very much to the fore here.

'Follow Me Follow'

Another one of the 'straight' tracks on this album again shows Jeff's burgeoning songwriting style, this song has a lovely use of melody, as well as the violin bow effect on his guitar again. The soaring strings and rising motifs fit in line with the lyrics about aeroplanes 'flying like birds'. Another familiar theme that starts to run through Jeff's later work are those of escape and wanting to be somewhere else, a concept he perfected on both ELO's *Eldorado* and *Time* albums. This wistfulness and romantic dreaming is another major theme of this album – 'escape' as a theme runs through it like the word 'Blackpool' runs through rock.

'Sitting In My Tree'

A jaunty almost 'Ob-La-Di Ob-La-Da' reggae shuffle provides the backdrop to this story about a chap who spends all day sitting in a tree, again juxtaposing the surreal with the normal. There is plenty of off-kilter lyricism mixed with straightforward music, and it's understandable that Jeff would have heard plenty of reggae in Birmingham due to the high number of Jamaican and Caribbean immigrants of the Windrush generation. What might nowadays get labelled cultural appropriating is here merely taking a familiar form of music and weaving it into the album's musical tapestry.

'On With The Show'

Mixing phasing and the musical hall style, this piano-driven little stomper seems almost like an interlude between the two sides of vinyl almost with a flourish and a welcome back after turning your record over, in *Sgt. Pepper* style. The brass and the production techniques of Offord and Chevin prevent this track from being merely filler.

'Lucky Man'

No, not the ELP track, this is another one of those nursery rhyme-type tracks, which seem to be quite simple at first listen. However, as you replay the song, you hear all the musical sound effects that appeared to have been borrowed from sound effect libraries, and a set of lyrics that seem to suggest the 'Lucky Man' in the title is anything but lucky. With a slightly unhinged vocal, this is probably the weakest track on the album.

'Mrs Ward'

With another one of Spencer's marching band beats, this is the cautionary tale of a mother who thinks she's doing the right thing in the army recruiting office. It has a memorable refrain and some more of those wonderfully plundered sound effects, as the song builds to its climax. The production of Offord and Chevin, working with Jeff Lynne, clearly works here, and with sound effects and tape loops, you can see why Offord went on to be so successful with Yes. It's great to see two big names who really impacted on 1970s music production cutting their teeth together on this early album.

'Pie In The Sky' (Pritchard)

The only song not written by Jeff Lynne, this is an up-tempo rocker, written and sung by Dave Pritchard. While most of the material here does have Lynne's unique stamp on it, here he takes a step back as Pritchard's rocker changes the mood of the album again, showing how successfully the tracks were sequenced. There is just about the right balance between the whimsy of some of the more music hall-style numbers, the bigger ballads and straight forward rockers.

'The Lady Who Said She Could Fly'

This is another track that foreshadows Lynne's future career direction, with soaring orchestral arrangements, plus his unique, almost plaintive, vocals and guitar sound. Again, this would fit right into a ELO set and no-one would bat an eyelid. The performance of the band and production make this lush and emotive, making this one of the stand out tracks on the album. 'Back To The Story' – the title of their career-defining set – comes from the lyrics to this song.

'End Of The Road'

An apt title for the last track on the album, this chiming song mixes the optimism of new beginnings, with hints of music hall in the whistling and the rag and bone percussion. The lyrics talk about waiting for the narrator as he'll be there 'at the end of the road' indicating another untold story. Are they eloping? Is he off to prison? We don't know, and that's part of the charm of these little vignettes.

Following on from the release of *The Birthday Party*, and despite its critical success, it was unsuccessful commercially. With Trevor Burton leaving The Move, in March 1969 Roy Wood invited Jeff Lynne to replace him. Jeff declined, and with a switch to the eight-track machines in Trident studios work started on their eponymous second album, trailered by a non-album single.

'Days Of The Broken Arrows' (Lynne) b/w 'Worn Red Carpet' (Pritchard)

Released on Liberty April 1969 in the UK only
Currently available on *Back To The Story*.... Parlophone 2007 and *The Birthday Party* expanded edition Grapefruit 2020
Personnel:
Jeff Lynne: vocals, guitar
Dave Pritchard: guitar, vocals
Greg Masters: bass guitar, vocals
Roger Spencer: drums, vocals

This single heralded a change in style for the band, with the music hall whimsy gone. Instead, there's a more driving guitar style with a slightly darker edge to it. The record was more reminiscent of how the musical landscape had shifted from the psychedelic to the harder rock sound as 1968 became 1969. With some harder guitar work, this was again a sign of Lynne's maturing songwriting craft and ability. Propelled by Spencer's drums and Masters bass, it contains some nifty progressive key changes on guitar and a straight forward edge to the lyrics. It's a triumph, and not only does it show how Lynne's songwriting was developing, but it also sounds like it could have fallen off either of the two Move albums he went to on to be involved in.

On the compilation Back to the Story and The Birthday Party expanded edition Grapefruit 2020 one of the bonus tracks is an alternative mix of 'Broken Arrows', with the opening part is switched with the bridge, creating an alternative version, showing how the song evolved to its final structure, changing the emphasis and focus of the song, and creating a harmonic pause before building back to its crescendo.

'Worn Red Carpet' is another Dave Pritchard original, with a darker tone to some of their earlier work. It was originally misprinted on the single label as 'Warm Red Carpet' but relates the story of the protagonist waking up on his worn red carpet. There is a faux Indian vibe to this, with the way the cadences change, and the guitar solos work, all continuing the subtle shift in direction for the band from their debut, their heavy touring schedule making the band's work here a lot tauter and rockier.

Like so many bands of this era, they had two different personalities, the harder rockier band that hit the road night after night, and the more refined 'polished' band that released the records and on these two songs, you can tell they are trying to marry up both facets, particularly as the technology of the day meant that they couldn't reproduce exactly on stage their studio work.

1969 saw one more single release in the UK, with 'Come with Me' backed with 'Reminds Me of You' which was released in July as a teaser for The Idle Race album, released in November 1969.

Idle Race (album)

Personnel:
Jeff Lynne: vocals, guitar
Dave Pritchard: guitar, vocals
Greg Masters: bass guitar, vocals
Roger Spencer: drums, vocals
(all songs by Jeff Lynne except where indicated)
Produced by Jeff Lynne and recorded at Trident studios
Released on Liberty records November 1969 (UK only) and currently available on
Back to the Story.... Parlophone 2007

Out of the two albums the Idle Race released with Jeff Lynne, this is my favourite. While *The Birthday Party* had its charm and originality, this is the album where Jeff really started to shape his songwriting, and it could be that during the recording of this album he spent a lot of time with Roy Wood. The Move's hit 'Blackberry Way', for instance, was demoed in Jeff's parents' front room in Shard End. This album is more coherent than its predecessor, and with Jeff producing he is starting to take control and shape the album. As such, it flows much better and builds to a satisfying musical conclusion, the final two tracks forming his first mini-epic.

Unfortunately, despite its strengths, the confidence of the band's performance, the maturity of Jeff Lynne's songwriting and his skilful production, the album again failed to set the world on fire. This is baffling when you listen to bands who made it bigger in the same era. Maybe it was a case of wrong place, wrong time for this line up of The Idle Race.

'Come With Me'
The albums lead single, this is an unashamedly commercial offering, influenced no doubt by the band's proximity to The Move and Roy Wood's knack for a killer tune. It sees The Idle Race making a bid for chart acceptance. Failing to even dent the charts, it's hummable melody, piano-driven riffs and upbeat

tempo nonetheless have a great summertime vibe. Yet this optimistic tune, with its doo-wop interlude and some great harmonies from the band, never caught the record buying public's attention, but as a calling card and way to open an album, it's a belter.

'Sea Of Dreams'

This gentle ballad has some lovely acoustic and slide guitar work, and is an example of how Lynne's production technique was honed, stripping away a lot of the sound effects from the previous record. Instead, we get a straight forward love song, and a wonderful musical coda. The song's harmony vocals and guitar riffs are repeated and embellished layer by layer by layer till it reaches its beautiful climax and for the first, but not the last time on this album, it segues straight into…

'Going Home'

This is probably the first song on a returning theme of Jeff's. It contains swelling strings, wonderfully bluesy guitar and in a plaintive theme about returning home, in which our narrator reminisces about what he's missing and where he's going, with the 13 July being very important. This is a vignette from a life, like those from the first album, but it's more complex, more personal, and paves the way for future narrators on ELO albums like the hero in *Time*.

'Reminds Me Of You' (Pritchard)

One of two Dave Pritchard tracks on the album, and with its classic rock style, and mournful lyrics about loss it brings the mood down. Pritchard's mournful vocals and the slower, understated beat, bring a different tone to the album. With some subtle guitar work, this track about love and loss, on first listen, seems to stand out like a sore thumb. However, after a few listens, it ties in with the loose themes on this album of love, loss and optimism. You must have the dark with the light and that's where this song fits beautifully.

'Mr Crow And Sir Norman'

Bringing us back up again is this jaunty ditty that echoes back to the debut album, with its tale about a runaway ventriloquist's dummy. Guest musician Mike Batt as one of three accordion players, all playing the same accordion at the same time. This is more mature than some of the songs on the debut but keeps Lynne's humour intact. It's that sense of humour and music hall pastiche that would follow through onto some of the less serious tracks by The Move like 'The Duke of Edinburgh's Lettuce' and 'My Marge'.

'Please No More Sad Songs'

Again, this is a gentler ballad, with an optimistic bittersweet melody and lyric. It also marks the point where Lynne really hits his stride. His careworn and beautiful vocals, which would go on to sing some of the greatest ballads and often-overlooked love songs of the 1970s, come into their own on here. The story of a girl who has left to find success is one he would return to again and again, refining and perfecting his bittersweet heartbreak, with the right balance of optimism and pathos. Despite the sad story here of the a lover gone, it's the happiness of the memories that shine through and are a reminder of why I love this song so much, and how much it means to me. It can make me weep and smile, and if that's not perfection in a pop song, I don't know what is.

'Girl At The Window'
This was the only song I'd heard from the band before I bought the *Back To The Story* set, and even then, that was only in a five-second snippet. In the early 1990s, there was a TV version of the Pete Frame's Rock Family Trees and in one episode it covered The Move and ELO. As a tiny footnote there was this picture of The Idle Race and a haunting little refrain 'John and Paul and Ringo and George, played their lovely tunes, as she sat in her room'. That was it. So, imagine how pleased I was to hear the full version. It starts off quite slowly and mournfully, before turning into a love song about a girl in her bedroom, who our narrator sees and fancies, but doesn't think he can reach. From a slow verse to an uplifting chorus, it changes from a ballad to a love song which is effective in its simplicity. There's no studio trickery – this is a wonderfully direct song that references Lynne's other big love, The Beatles.

'Big Chief Woolley Bosher'
Where do I start with this one? Jeff Lynne seems to have a Wild West infatuation, one which he taps into far better on 'Wild West Hero' from ELO's 'Out of the Blue'. However, this song tells the story of how the western settlers stole the Indian's land. It is almost a bit too clichéd, and with its pseudo chants and mock Indian drumming might have had good intentions, but it seems unable to decide whether it's all serious or meant to be taken in a tongue in cheek sort of way. While it might have been made with the best intentions at the time and the production is excellent, it doesn't stand up to much scrutiny now.

'Someone Knocking' (Pritchard)
The second of the Pritchard originals on this album, this song has a Dave Davies (of the Kinks) vibe to it. Its rockabilly sound and echoey effects turn it from what could be a run of the mill rocker into something that is a little bit off-kilter. It has a percussive groove, and some funky rock and roll guitar from Pritchard and Lynne, both of whom would use that rock n' roll pastiche style to greater effect on later songs. It is an upbeat song before leading into the closing two tracks.

'A Better Life (The Weatherman Knows)'
This could be considered Jeff Lynne's first mini-epic, inasmuch as 'A Better Life' segues into the next song, 'Hurry Up John', making them almost a single piece. 'A Better Life (The Weatherman Knows)', is a piano-driven ballad, one of the first

to feature a regular motif of Jeff's writing, the concept of change (a precursor to his 'Concerto For A Rainy Day' from *Out Of The Blue*). It has some wonderfully heartfelt lyrics, and a beautifully understated performance from the band, plus a little bit of piano boogie and that mythical weatherman – not the last time third party characters would appear in Jeff's writing.

'Hurry Up John'

We then segue into the rocking 'Hurry Up John', with its chanting verses straight from the football terraces. Lynne comes in with an insistent, nagging riff, big beats and fuzzy solos and there are plenty of multi-part harmonies as the band rocket through this song. The way these two songs are structured is pretty much a blueprint for the way Jeff Lynne's songwriting would develop in The Move and brings this second album to a close with style and confidence.

Jeff Leaves

When Roy Wood asked Jeff Lynne to join The Move in January 1970, he agreed. With the loss of their main songwriter, The Idle Race might have have folded. Instead, they recruited Mike Hopkins on guitar and vocals and Dave Walker (later of Savoy Brown, Fleetwood Mac, and ever so briefly, Black Sabbath) on vocals and harmonica. The band continued into the early 1970s, releasing two singles in 1970.

'In The Summertime' (Dorset) b/w 'Told You Twice' (Pritchard)

Personnel:
Mike Hopkins: vocals, guitar
Dave Pritchard: guitar, vocals
Greg Masters: bass guitar, vocals
Roger Spencer: drums, vocals
Dave Walker: harmonica, vocals
Produced by Noel Walker
Released on Liberty Records 1970 (overseas territories only never released in the UK or the US)
Currently available on *Back To The Story*.... Parlophone 2007

Despite not being released in either the UK or the US, this note by note cover version of 'In The Summertime' got to number one in Argentina, as well as hitting the charts in Germany. Their version adds nothing much to the original and does seem very like a holding exercise for a band who were searching for their identity. Pritchard's 'Told you Twice', however, is a wonderful piece of rock and blues, with some great skiffle drumming from Spencer and some lovely bluesy guitar from Hopkins and Pritchard. The change of direction is obvious as it eschews the quirkiness of the Lynne era, heading towards to a more straight-forward blues-rock sound.

'Neanderthal Man' (Godley, Crème, Stewart) / **'Victim Of Circumstance'** (Pritchard)
Personnel:
Mike Hopkins: vocals, guitar
Dave Pritchard: guitar, vocals
Greg Masters: bass guitar, vocals
Roger Spencer:- drums, vocals
Dave Walker: harmonica, vocals
Produced by Noel Walker
Released on Liberty Records in Canada 1970
Currently available on *Back to the Story...* Parlophone 2007

For the band's second single of 1970, The Idle Race took on the powerful percussive tones of Hotlegs and their pre-10CC hit, recording a note for note cover version. This time though, because it's got the 10CC hallmark all over it, it's a far more appropriate tune than 'In the Summertime', and the band sound like they're having fun recording it.

Once again, it's the B-side that is more interesting here, with the Pritchard-penned 'Victim of Circumstance' being another great track. Having stepped up as the main songwriter on Lynne's departure, Pritchard doesn't disappoint. His forte was far more rock and blues-based than Lynne's was initially, and the move away from symphonic pop is the biggest difference in the post-Lynne line-up. With some great bluesy riffing, and Walker's soulful vocals, this is where The Idle Race Mk II hit their stride and came into their own. The Idle Race story did not end when Jeff Lynne left, and this track is proof that they still had a lot to offer. It's one of their best, with a mellow, bluesy feel, some great guitar work, and – as ever – the power of Roger Spencer driving it on.

Time Is (album)
Personnel:
Mike Hopkins: vocals, lead guitar, acoustic guitar
Dave Pritchard: rhythm guitar, vocals, flute
Greg Masters: bass guitar, vocals, electric cello
Roger Spencer: drums, percussion, vocals
Dave Walker: harmonica, vocals, piano
Produced by the Idle Race and Kenneth Young
Released on Regal Zonophone May 1971 (UK Only)
Currently available on *Back to the Story....* Parlophone 2007

As a fan of early 1970's music, the band's third album *Time Is* is one of my favourites from this era, sounding nothing like its predecessor. It mixes folk with prog and rock and is a radical departure from the pop sound with Jeff Lynne as Dave Prichard became the main writer. As often happens, one

119

wonders if they might have picked up a new audience had they changed their name for this record, as it is so completely different to what went before. As the bands last recorded statement, *Time Is* wasn't the most coherent album ever made, but it's still an excellent one.

'Dancing Flower' (Pritchard)
This lively opener to the album manages to blend both folk and prog in one fell swoop, with the flute of Pritchard making its appearance here on the record. The 'fa la la' vocals and village green imagery, still manage to evoke the more sinister 'wyrd folk' music played on the soundtrack to the film *The Wicker Man*. For anyone expecting more of the same style from the band, it's one hell of a surprise as an opener and not a bad one either.

'Sad O'Sad' (Pritchard)
A more funky blues-driven piece than its predecessor, this song features more harmony vocals and is a more straight forward love song from Pritchard. The guitar solo from Hopkins is impressive, and the folky intro, as well as the two guitars duelling, are reminiscent of Wishbone Ash, as both Spencer and Masters bounce off each other, allowing room for the guitars to do their work.

'The Clock' (Pritchard)
The tempo slows a bit for this Pritchard ballad, with some mournful harmonica from Walker, and some emotive vocals. The song builds and builds into a lament for a lost love, again with some wonderful guitar work and powerful vocals from Walker, whose soulful blues voice really suits the style of writing.

'I Will See You' (Walker)
This is once more a more acoustic, folk driven track, reminiscent of the work of The Strawbs or Magna Carta, with a simple, percussive acoustic guitar sound, subtle percussion from Spencer and the lilt of Pritchard's flute. The band's wonderful harmony vocals, always a strength and very much underrated, help build this song, as Master's cello underpins the haunting refrain. What could have been a very simple piece, subtly and slowly builds with a wonderful acoustic guitar and flute coda rounding off one of the highpoints so far on this album

'By The Sun' (Spencer)
This is the longest song the band recorded, at 6:42, and it is a Spencer original. There are some ominous Indian guitar effects and vocals that build and weave in tune with the song. The acoustic instruments are put to bed, and the full electric band come out to play on this, as, like so many tracks on this album it builds and builds to a musical crescendo. The lead guitar of Hopkins weaves and ebbing before evoking a renaissance fayre, with some folk-rock flourishes. It does go over the top, but the band clearly relishing getting their teeth into it

and the musicianship is totally wonderful. If a band couldn't self-indulge every so often, then it wouldn't be a record from 1971!

'Alcatraz' (Pritchard, Spencer, Walker)
This is not a holiday destination anyone would like to go, but as song subject it's emotive and here it's a powerfully funky driving piece of rock. It has some great vocals, percussive beats and a meaty guitar riff. This is the first proper rock out on the album and I can't help thinking it would have been a slightly better record with a little bit more straightforward rock on it. The guitar solos are sublime – they have really got their groove on this one – and you can't help but enjoy the funk as they drive some great big riffs through the middle of the song.

'And The Rain' (Walker, Pritchard)
This is another acoustically-driven folk song, reminiscent of the Strawbs or Lindisfarne, with its storytelling-style of songwriting. The acoustic guitar weaves around the electric and the chorus is very catchy. The fingerpicking solo and harmonica work is wonderful and had the song been picked up by the radio, it would surely have been a bit of a hit, as it has all the hallmarks of a great single. It's a wonderful piece of folk-pop.

'She Sang Hymns Out Of Tune' (Jesse Lee Kincaid)
The first cover version on the album is the band's take on a song by Californian legend Jesse Lee Kincaid. This version is another great piece of electric folk, with some wonderful harmony vocals, and some outstanding guitar work from both Hopkins and Pritchard. Again, this shows the direction in which the band were heading; the emphasis very much on that area in-between folk and rock, where other bands like the Lindisfarne or Strawbs were setting out their stall. The difficulty with this album, though, is that it isn't sure whether the band is a folk-rock band, a progressive rock group or a straightforward rock outfit. While there was always that split element between a live band and an album band, this schizophrenic element sometimes makes the change in styles jarring, while at other times it flows perfectly.

'Bitter Green' (Gordon Lightfoot)
This cover of the Gordon Lightfoot song flows on perfectly from the previous song, the tempo, the style, the mood all working together. The mid-tempo beats and harmony vocals blend the acoustic with the electric perfectly. Some sublime musical interplay between the band members and some fantastic guitar work makes this one of the more successful cover versions on the album.

'We Want It All' (Walker, Spencer)
With some electric piano and shuffling drums and harmony vocals, this track flows perfectly again from the previous song, proving when the band get it

right, they get it bang on.

With a chanting chorus and it's pared-down instrumentation, it has elements of South African musician John Kongos' proto-glam style. This song is a call to arms, a rallying cry to get what you want, and it's underpinned by a subtle piano riff and some funky percussion, before breaking down into another funky section with driving harmony vocals. This is one of the best songs on the album and really takes the band out of safe territory. Indeed, a few more songs like this would have benefitted the album, with its innovative instrumentation, and driving guitar work. It sounds intentionally chaotic, and the counter melodies and the solo that the build-up to a crescendo that makes the track work so well.

The End of The Idle Race

After more personnel changes and no further records, the band eventually morphed into The Steve Gibbons band, joined by Trevor Burton from The Move, which again shows how intertwined these bands from Birmingham's were. But that was the brief recorded output of The Idle Race, a band who always appear as a footnote in most musical history books, but who deserve a lot more time and a lot more space of their own, not just by launching the career of Jeff Lynne as he headed off to The Move, but by producing several classic songs in their own right.

The Who - *on track*

every album, every song

The Who - on track
every album, every song
Geoffrey Feakes
Paperback
176 pp
42 colour photographs
978-1-78952-076-7
£14.99
USD 21.95

Every album produced by one of the world's best-selling - and most controversial - rock bands.

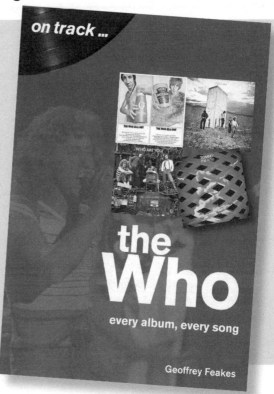

Formed in 1964 and still going strong in 2020, the Who are one of the most popular and enduring bands in the history of rock. The legendary debut album *My Generation* and a string of hit singles paved the way for Live At Leeds, hailed as the best live rock album of all time, and the best selling *Who's Next*. Powered by the phenomenal rhythm section of Keith Moon and John Entwistle, they earned a reputation as a premier live act and pioneered festival and arena performances. The rock operas *Tommy* and *Quadrophenia* took popular music into uncharted territories and both inspired hit films. Despite regular infighting, breakups and the death of two key members, the band continued into the 21st century with the well received *Endless Wire* album and original members Roger Daltrey and Pete Townshend stage spectacular live shows to this day.

This book examines each one of the band's studio albums, including the latest Who released in December 2019. Non-album tracks are also included and the book traces the band's long and diverse history. Compilations, live albums and soundtracks are also discussed, making this the most comprehensive guide to the music of the Who yet published. Whether the reader is a diehard fan or someone curious to see what lies beyond *Tommy*, this is essential reading.

10cc - *on track*

every album, every song

10cc and Godley and Creme -
on track
every album, every song
Peter Kearns
Paperback
176 pages
42 colour photographs
978-1-78952-054-5
US ISBN: 978-1-78952-075-0
£14.99
USD 21.95

**Every album
produced by this cult
British band - and
offshoot duo Kevin
Godley and Lol
Creme.**

Hailing from Manchester, England, sophisticated pop purveyors 10cc hit the ground running with their 1972 debut single, 'Donna'. Their pedigree reached back to bassist Graham Gouldman's '60s' songwriting successes including The Yardbirds' 'For Your Love' and The Hollies' 'Bus Stop'. Guitarist and recording engineer, Eric Stewart, was already a bonafide pop star having sung the global 1966 hit, 'Groovy Kind of Love', for his group The Mindbenders. When the pair teamed up with drummer/singer Kevin Godley and multi-instrumentalist/singer, Lol Creme, the combination wrought a legacy of four albums. They included the ambitious *The Original Soundtrack* and several hit singles, including the groundbreaking 'I'm Not In Love,' that were rich in eclectic boundary-pushing pop that earned 10cc comparisons to The Beatles while still occupying a unique position in music.

Departing in 1976, Godley and Creme moved on to create genre-defying experimental albums, while Gouldman and Stewart continued their run of hit singles and albums with a new 10cc lineup. Their final album was 1995's, *Mirror Mirror*, a highly respectable full stop on the influential band's colourful and innovative discography. This book examines every released recording by both Godley & Creme and 10cc, including the band's debut album under their early name, Hotlegs.

Mike Oldfield - *on track*

every album, every song

Mike Oldfield - on track
every album, every song
Ryan Yard
Paperback
176 pages
42 colour photographs
978-1-78952-060-6
£14.99
USD 21.95

Every album produced by one of the most enigmatic and talented solo artists of the 1970s.

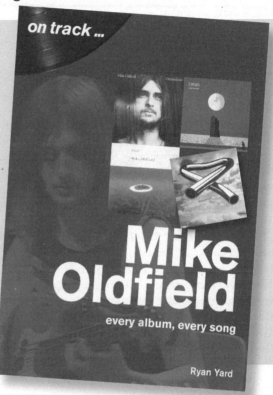

It can be difficult for an artist to have such overwhelming success so early into their career as was the case for Mike Oldfield. To this day, his name is forever synonymous with the album *Tubular Bells*. Mike followed this album with three further long form works in the 1970s, before venturing off onto other musical paths. The 1980s saw further success both in the albums and singles charts, while recent years have seen a return to long form music, often via sequels to his most famous work, with his most recent album being *Return To Ommadawn* in 2017.

The music of Mike Oldfield touches listeners in ways that can be hard to describe. It bridges the gap between many musical cultures, whilst staying sharp and alert to current technological trends. In this book, Ryan Yard looks at the entire catalogue of albums to uncover what it is that makes his music so special. Each track from every album is critiqued with the aim of offering long term fans a different perspective whilst enticing new fans to explore and familiarise themselves with such wonderful new music. It makes a wonderful companion as the listener absorbs the music, hopefully offering food for thought as they embark on, or continue, their journey through the music of this remarkable artist.

On Track series

Queen – Andrew Wild 978-1-78952-003-3
Emerson Lake and Palmer – Mike Goode 978-1-78952-000-2
Deep Purple and Rainbow 1968-79 – Steve Pilkington 978-1-78952-002-6
Yes – Stephen Lambe 978-1-78952-001-9
Blue Oyster Cult – Jacob Holm-Lupo 978-1-78952-007-1
The Beatles – Andrew Wild 978-1-78952-009-5
Roy Wood and the Move – James R Turner 978-1-78952-008-8
Genesis – Stuart MacFarlane 978-1-78952-005-7
Jethro Tull – Jordan Blum 978-1-78952-016-3
The Rolling Stones 1963-80 – Steve Pilkington 978-1-78952-017-0
Judas Priest – John Tucker 978-1-78952-018-7
Toto – Jacob Holm-Lupo 978-1-78952-019-4
Van Der Graaf Generator – Dan Coffey 978-1-78952-031-6
Frank Zappa 1966 to 1979 – Eric Benac 978-1-78952-033-0
Elton John in the 1970s – Peter Kearns 978-1-78952-034-7
The Moody Blues – Geoffrey Feakes 978-1-78952-042-2
The Beatles Solo 1969-1980 – Andrew Wild 978-1-78952-030-9
Steely Dan – Jez Rowden 978-1-78952-043-9
Hawkwind – Duncan Harris 978-1-78952-052-1
Fairport Convention – Kevan Furbank 978-1-78952-051-4
Iron Maiden – Steve Pilkington 978-1-78952-061-3
Dream Theater – Jordan Blum 978-1-78952-050-7
10CC and Godley and Crème – Peter Kearns 978-1-78952-054-5
Gentle Giant – Gary Steel 978-1-78952-058-3
Kansas – Kevin Cummings 978-1-78952-057-6
Mike Oldfield – Ryan Yard 978-1-78952-060-6
The Who – Geoffrey Feakes 978-1-78952-076-7
Crosby, Stills and Nash – Andrew Wild 978-1-78952-039-2
U2 – Eoghan Lyng 978-1-78952-078-1
Barclay James Harvest – Keith and Monika Domone 978-1-78952-067-5
Steve Hackett – Geoffrey Feakes 978-1-78952-098-9
Renaissance – David Detmer 978-1-78952-062-0
Dire Straits – Andrew Wild 978-1-78952-044-6
Camel – Hamish Kuzminski 978-1-78952-040-8
Rush – Will Romano 978-1-78952-080-4
Joni Mitchell – Peter Kearns 978-1-78952-081-1
UFO – Richard James 978-1-78952-073-6
Kate Bush – Bill Thomas 978-1-78952-097-2
Asia – Pete Braidis 978-1-78952-099-6
Aimee Mann – Jez Rowden 978-1-78952-036-1
Pink Floyd Solo – Mike Goode 978-1-78952-046-0
Gong – Kevan Furbank 978-1-78952-082-8

Decades Series
Pink Floyd in the 1970s – Georg Purvis 978-1-78952-072-9
Marillion in the 1980s – Nathaniel Webb 978-1-78952-065-1
Focus in the 1970s – Stephen Lambe 978-1-78952-079-8
Curved Air in the 1970s – Laura Shenton 978-1-78952-069-9

On Screen series
Carry On... – Stephen Lambe 978-1-78952-004-0
Seinfeld Seasons 1 to 5 – Stephen Lambe 978-1-78952-012-5
Monty Python – Steve Pilkington 978-1-78952-047-7
Doctor Who: The David Tennant Years – Jamie Hailstone 978-1-78952-066-8
James Bond – Andrew Wild 978-1-78952-010-1
David Cronenberg – Patrick Chapman 978-1-78952- 071-2

Other Books
Maximum Darkness – Deke Leonard 978-1-78952-048-4
The Twang Dynasty – Deke Leonard 978-1-78952-049-1
Tommy Bolin: In and Out of Deep Purple – Laura Shenton 978-1-78952-070-5
Jon Anderson and the Warriors - the road to Yes – David Watkinson 978-1-78952-059-0
Derek Taylor: For Your Radioactive Children - Andrew Darlington 978-1-78952-038-5
20 Walks Around Tewkesbury – Stephen Lambe 978-1-78952-074-3

and many more to come!

Would you like to write for Sonicbond Publishing?

We are mainly a music publisher, but we also occasionally publish in other genres including film and television. At Sonicbond Publishing we are always on the look-out for authors, particularly for our two main series.

On Track. Mixing fact with in depth analysis, the On Track series examines the entire recorded work of a particular musical artist or group. All genres are considered from easy listening and jazz to 60s soul to 90s pop, via rock and metal.

Decades. This series singles out a particular decade in an artist or group's history and focuses on that decade in more detail than may be allowed in the On Track series.

While professional writing experience would, of course, be an advantage, the most important qualification is to have real enthusiasm and knowledge of your subject. First-time authors are welcomed, but the ability to write well in English is essential.

Sonicbond Publishing has distribution throughout Europe and North America, and all our books are also published in E-book form. Authors will be paid a royalty based on sales of their book. Further details about our books are available from www.sonicbondpublishing.com. To contact us, complete the contact form there or email info@sonicbondpublishing.co.uk